Technology, Education—Connections
The TEC Series

Series Editor: Marcia C. Linn
Advisory Board: Robert Bjork, Chris Dede,
Carol Lee, Jim Minstrell, Jonathan Osborne, Mitch Resnick

Learning in the Cloud

How (and Why) to Transform
Schools with Digital Media

MARK WARSCHAUER

FOREWORD BY CHRIS DEDE

Teachers College, Columbia University
New York and London

Published by Teachers College Press, 1234 Amsterdam Avenue, New York, NY 10027

Figure 2.2 reprinted with kind permission from Springer Science+Business Media: *Second International Handbook of Educational Change*, 2009, p. 829, Adaptive people and adaptive systems: Issues of learning and design, Bransford, J., Mosborg, S., Copland, M. A., Honig, M. A., Nelson, H. G., Gawel, D. et al.

Library of Congress Cataloging-in-Publication Data

Warschauer, Mark.
  Learning in the cloud : how (and why) to transform schools with digital media / Mark Warschauer ; foreword by Chris Dede.
    p. cm.—(Technology, Education—Connections: The TEC Series)
  Includes bibliographical references and index.
    ISBN 978-0-8077-5249-4 (pbk.)—ISBN 978-0-8077-5250-0 (hardcover) 1. Educational technology. 2. Education—Effect of technological innovations on. 3. Education—Computer-assisted instruction. 4. Digital media. I. Title.
  LB1028.3.W35 2011
  371.33—dc23
                                                                    2011017736
ISBN 978-0-8077-5249-4 (paper)
ISBN 978-0-8077-5250-0 (hardcover)

Printed on acid-free paper
Manufactured in the United States of America

18 17 16 15 14 13 12 11   8 7 6 5 4 3 2 1

Contents

Foreword

This important book addresses a core challenge for K–12 schooling: How can we implement modern interactive media to realize gains in educational outcomes comparable to the major increases in effectiveness that information and communication technologies (ICT) have accomplished in every other sector of society? As Mark Warschauer discusses, society has made large investments in learning technologies that, on average, have produced few results—even though shining illustrations exist of sophisticated usage resulting in substantial improvements. Rather than retry the same failed approaches with newer technologies and more resources, a different model of how ICT increases improvement in learning and teaching is needed, from which more successful implementation strategies can emerge. This volume describes why "conventional wisdom" about investments in educational technology is flawed, offers a research-based conceptual framework as an alternative, and provides detailed evidence of the practicality and power of this model.

Warschauer's ideas are particularly important at this time in the history of education. The industrial-era structure for schooling is collapsing: Countries can no longer afford expensive, labor-intensive social services delivered ineffectively. What was an excellent education for the 1980s is woefully inadequate for the 21st century. Pervasive inequities are too often reinforced rather than redressed by schooling, leading to huge costs later in life for both the victims and society. At a time when difficult financial, ecological, and military issues overshadow civilization, our school systems are throwing away much of the human talent in the next generation, minds and hearts that are desperately needed to steer through the chaotic, dangerous decades looming ahead.

In looking for leverage on these crucial challenges, learning technologies offer great promise. Few other innovations in education speak as broadly and deeply to 21st-century problems—and opportunities. Warschauer's model is consistent with the conceptual frameworks and strategies espoused in the U.S. Department of Education's 2010 National

Educational Technology Plan (NETP). This Plan articulates a vision, based on theory and evidence, of 21st-century education powered by ICT. The major themes in the NETP (Learning, Assessment, Teaching, Infrastructure, Productivity, and Research) are all richly interwoven in *Learning in the Cloud*. In particular, Warschauer's model exemplifies a core principle in the NETP: "Engaging and effective learning experiences can be individualized or differentiated for particular learners . . . or personalized, which combines paced and tailored learning with flexibility in content or theme designed to fit the interests and prior experience of each learner" (U.S. Department of Education, 2010, pp. 11–12).

Warschauer's model also instantiates key strategies for assessment espoused in the NETP articulates: "When students are learning online, there are multiple opportunities to exploit the power of technology for formative assessment. . . . As students work, the system can capture their inputs and collect evidence of their problem-solving sequences, knowledge, and strategy use, as reflected by the information each student selects or inputs, the number of attempts they make, the number of hints and feedback given, and the time allocation across parts of the problem" (U.S. Department of Education, 2010, pp. 29–30).

Finally, *Learning in the Cloud* provides detailed, practical examples of the type of connected teaching the NETP champions, which "offers a vast array of opportunities to personalize learning. Many simulations and models for use in science, history, and other subject areas are now available online. . . . To deeply engage their students, educators need to know about their students' goals and interests and have knowledge of learning resources and systems that can help students plan sets of learning experiences that are personally meaningful" (U.S. Department of Education, 2010, pp. 41–42).

Where the NETP sketches a blueprint, this book provides case-based illustrations of these ideas in practice. Warschauer's detailed strategies are invaluable to districts seeking to leverage learning technologies effectively for transformation at scale. This book is much needed as we seek 21st-century structures for education that transcend the obsolescence of industrial-era schooling.

—*Chris Dede*
Harvard Graduate School of Education

REFERENCE

U.S. Department of Education. (2010). *Transforming American education: Learning powered by technology*. Washington, DC: Office of Educational Technology, U.S. Department of Education. http://www.ed.gov/technology/netp-2010

Preface

K–12 education has been among the slowest sectors of society to fully integrate digital media. It is time for that to change. Outside of schools, almost nobody conducts research, analyzes data, carries out a scientific experiment, or writes an in-depth paper without use of an Internet-connected computer or digital device. In school, we can teach students to do these important things a lot better if they have the right tools for the job.

And change is coming. The student-computer ratio in U.S. schools has already fallen over the last 2 decades and is down to about 3 to 1 (Gray, Thomas, & Lewis, 2010a). With the advent of low-cost netbooks and tablets, the availability of open access and cloud-based resources, and the growing digitalization of educational content and assessments, the question may soon change from how we can afford to replace textbooks and paper with digital media to how we can afford *not* to. It is easy to imagine a day in the not-too-distant future when each student will have an individual computer or digital device in a typical U.S. classroom.

The accelerating availability of digital media in schools, including devices, software, and content, raises exciting possibilities. A child can use a wireless laptop, netbook, or tablet to access interactive and individualized instructional material; collect and analyze data for research projects; write, revise, and publish papers; communicate and collaborate across the school or the world; and use or create multimedia games, simulations, and computer programs. Yet, digital devices do not generate learning simply by being handed to a child. As a blogger (Legionzero, 2009) put it, "My 6 year old nephew can sit at the computer for hours and if no one guides him all he takes away from those hours is the ability to cross the finish line with a gorilla on top of a go-cart."

It takes more than handing a child a netbook or iPad to transform education. Such transformation requires clear goals about what digital media in schools can achieve; the appropriate curricula, pedagogy, and assessment to reach these goals; and the right social and technical infrastructure to support the endeavor. In short, we have to see that through use of digital media, students become both *untethered* (free to pursue educational content and interests within and beyond their textbooks inside and outside of schools) and *connected* (to the goals, environments, networks, content, and support structures that will allow them to thrive as learners).

This book will explain how. Although other works have addressed similar topics, this book takes a unique approach. First, while much discussion of digital media and learning is speculative, this book distills the key lessons from a broad range of research, including scores of studies on technology and learning published by others as well as our own case-study research of one-to-one (one computer per student) programs with laptops, netbooks, tablets, and handheld devices from 2003 to 2010 carried out in a dozen school districts in Maine, California, Colorado, Alabama, and Mexico. During this time, our team spent more than 1,500 hours observing classes in 20 schools; interviewed 300 teachers, parents, students, and staff; surveyed 3,500 students and 100 teachers; and analyzed test-score outcomes for 5,000 students in English language arts, mathematics, and other subjects. We have examined technology use in a wide range of educational contexts, from 1st grade through 12th, in wealthy suburban schools and impoverished urban ones, and with students in regular, gifted, special needs, and English language learner programs. Through our selection of schools and teachers to study, we have examined both typical practices as well as those that are especially interesting to learn from. (To acknowledge the outstanding teachers we have observed and interviewed, all names of teachers and schools in this book are real, except when otherwise specified.)

Second, most books on technology in education are written from either a utopian perspective, promising radical reform through access to digital media, or a dystopian view, warning that schools have never changed and never will. Although I am optimistic about the potential of technology to transform learning, I am also realistic about the enormous infrastructural and educational challenges required to make meaningful change happen. This book combines a positive vision of what can be accomplished with technology with a hardheaded perspective of how to bring that vision to fruition.

Finally, there is a great deal of conventional wisdom that too often goes unchallenged by proponents of technology in the classroom. Overcoming a digital divide, promoting 21st-century skills, and teachers becoming a guide on the side are just three of the mantras one often hears about technology and learning. This book critically evaluates these and other concepts to explain whether and how they can effectively guide educational reform.

Acknowledgments

I am deeply indebted to the contributions of those who funded these studies, collaborated in the research, and invited our research team into their schools. Funders include the National Science Foundation (Discovery Research K–12, NSF Rapid Grant #1053767, Interactive Science and Technology Instruction for English Learners), the Haynes Foundation, Google Research Awards, the Episcopal Church of the Diocese of Los Angeles, the University of California Institute for Mexico and the United States, the Ada Byron Research Center for Diversity in Computing & Information Technology, and the Cultural Diversity Studies program of the UC Irvine Academic Senate Council on Research. Collaborators include Kathleen Arada, Kelly Bruce, Vanitha Chandrasekhar, Penelope Collins, Melissa Courtney, Thurston Domina, George Farkas, Doug Grimes, David Hernandez, David Lee, Sonja Lind, Jason Lu, Julia Nyberg, Kylie Peppler, Ying Ren, Michele Rousseau, LaWanna Shelton, Kurt Suhr, Jorge Velastegui, Bryan Ventura, Melanie Wade, Paige Ware, Lisa Woo, and Binbin Zheng. Educators who have been of assistance are too numerous to name, but I am especially grateful to Tony Anderson, Susan Astarita, David Grant, Jim Klein, Joan Lucid, Dan Maas, Bette Manchester, Cameron McCune, Jenith Mishne, Jackie Pearce, David Silvernail, and Michael Wilson. Finally, I thank my wife, Keiko, and our children, Danny, Mika, and Noah, whose own passions about learning with technology inspire me every day.

1

Introduction

Music is not in the piano.

—Alan Kay (1991, p. 138)

Throughout the United States, immigrant students and English language learners often start a dangerous decline in the upper elementary grades, when increasing literacy challenges lead to a "4th-grade slump" in reading and writing from which they never academically recover (Chall & Jacobs, 2003). Not so in Littleton Public Schools outside Denver, where students at the district's special school for English learners use blogs, wikis, and other social media to hone their writing skills, strengthen their sense of connection to school, and narrow the gap between their academic performance and that of their peers.

These benefits are the results of an instructional program involving individual computer access launched in the district in 2008–2009. The program was developed and planned to support a new curricular initiative for improved writing and literacy. Professional development was carried out to ensure that principals and teachers understood the nature of the curriculum and the role of technology in it. Detailed attention was paid in selecting the hardware and software for the project to ensure that they matched well with curricular objectives at the lowest possible cost. An inexpensive netbook using open source software was chosen, to be used in conjunction with free cloud-based and online resources.

The 1st-year pilot program carried out in 5th grade was carefully evaluated and found to be successful on a number of benchmarks established by the district, so funds were raised to expand the program to 6th and 9th grade. Appropriate grade-level curriculum was developed for the middle and high school levels, and additional professional development was carried out. The 2nd-year implementation was also very successful as indicated by test scores, teacher and student reports, and independent evaluation, and the district gained national acclaim for the program (e.g.,

Gabriel, 2010). Further fundraising was carried out, allowing for expansion the following year to all grades from 5th to 10th.

Birmingham Public Schools in Alabama took a very different path in implementing a laptop program. Like in Littleton, Birmingham schools used low-cost netbook computers and open source software, but the similarity ends there.

The Birmingham program was initiated not by the school district, but by the mayor and president of the City Council after they became attracted to the international One Laptop per Child program (for an overview of OLPC, see Warschauer & Ames, 2010). OLPC was launched in 2005 with the goal of distributing and producing a $100 laptop to children in developing countries (Kraemer, Dedrick, & Sharma, 2009). Its founder, Nicholas Negroponte, believes that if they are provided with OLPC's specially designed XO laptops, children can teach not only themselves but also their family members, without regard to curriculum development, pedagogy, teacher training, or other infrastructure, and without pilot programs, staged implementation, or evaluation. As Negroponte (2009) explains:

> I'd like you to imagine that I told you "I have a technology that is going to change the quality of life." Then I tell you "Really the right thing to do is to set up a pilot project to test my technology. Then the second thing to do is once the pilot has been running for some period of time is to go and measure very carefully the benefits of that technology." Then I am to tell you that we are going to do is very scientifically evaluate this technology, with control groups—giving it to some, giving it to others. This all is very reasonable until I tell you the technology is electricity, and you say "Wait, you don't have to do that." But you don't have to do that with laptops and learning either. The fact that somebody in the room would say the impact is unclear is to me amazing—unbelievably amazing.

In 2008, Birmingham mayor Larry Langford contacted Negroponte about bringing OLPC to Alabama. Langford and the City Council president, John Katopodis, proposed a new sales tax to purchase 15,000 XOs, which would be handed over to children in grades 1 to 5, in accordance with OLPC principles. Echoing themes that Negroponte has expressed, Langford explained his motivation for the program:

> We need to put a laptop in each child's hands and step back and let them learn about the world and use their brilliant minds to come up with solutions to the world's problems. If we give them these XOs and get out of their way, they'll be teaching us about the world. How many of us have questions about a computer and ask someone who is older how to fix it? None of us! You find the youngest person in the room and they'll have it

fixed in a second. These kids get it, and we need to give them the tools that
they'll need to succeed. That tool is the XO laptop. (Education Initiatives,
2008, n. pag)

School district officials had many hesitations about the proposed program, including the lack of funding devoted to curriculum development
or teacher training, the lack of Internet access in most Birmingham elementary schools, and the proposed use of a laptop that was created for
developing countries rather than for U.S. classrooms. In line with Negroponte's vision, Langford proposed that all 15,000 computers be distributed at once, without any pilot program, something the school district
also resisted. Finally, after Langford threatened to pass out the computers
to children from trucks in parking lots if the school district would not
cooperate, a compromise was reached in which the program would proceed districtwide following a short 6-week pilot program in one school
in spring 2009. The remaining laptops were distributed to children in fall
2009.

Although students received the laptops with enthusiasm, the program quickly ran into trouble. A pre-post student survey showed that
70% of the laptops had technical problems in the first 6 months, leaving
many of them inoperable (Warschauer & Ames, 2010). More than 80%
of students reported that they used the laptops little or never in school.
Teachers in the district showed so little interest in the program that a survey of teachers had to be cancelled due to low response rate.

My visit to a school in December 2009, some 19 months after the
program was launched, shed more light on the program's difficulties. Although the school I visited was selected by the district administration—
indeed, it was the only Birmingham school I was permitted to visit in
the district since others were reportedly having greater difficulties with
implementing the laptop program—there appeared to be little laptop use
at the school. In the classes I observed, only 40% of students had working
laptops with them; most of the remaining students told me that their laptops were no longer functioning. (One student asked pleadingly if I could
fix his XO; he apparently hadn't read the message from the mayor claiming that nobody ever asks anybody older to fix a computer.) Two students
were handpicked out of the entire school for personal interviews with
me. Although they both adored their XOs, neither had a working laptop
with them. One told me that hers was broken and the other said she
stopped bringing it because her teacher didn't make use of the laptops.

Although the school was reportedly wired for Internet access—one of
the only elementary schools in Birmingham with that capacity—a teacher
told me that her students sometimes had to go to the hallway to get a
connection. Other teachers complained that the sluggish performance of

the laptops and their lack of connections to printers or servers made them difficult to integrate in instruction; indeed, to read and respond to student writing, teachers had to walk around student by student to look at each individual screen. The 2 hours of paid training provided to teachers could barely scratch the surface of how to use the XO's unusual interface, much less how to deploy the laptop for teaching and learning. Only a handful of teachers appeared to be using the laptops at the school, and mostly in limited ways, other than one teacher who had set up an afterschool club for visual programming with software called Scratch (see Chapter 3).

The pre-post survey showed that students with working laptops used them at home, but with disappointing results (Warschauer, Cotton, & Ames, 2010). Prior to getting the XOs, most students in Birmingham already had access to computers outside of school, either through home ownership by their family or at the local library. The survey found that the students' use of computers for academic or content creation purposes diminished after they received the XOs. Specifically, the frequency with which students used a computer to create or listen to podcasts, do research, or do homework all decreased significantly from the pre-survey (before XO ownership) to the post-survey (after XO ownership), as did the percentage of students who reported that they created a Web page or shared creations online. However, there was a significant increase following ownership of the XOs for chat room use and instant messaging. The amount of students' computer anxiety also increased from pre- to post-survey, and the percentage of students who said they wanted to go to college decreased.

Finally, although the total cost per unit for hardware and software (about $200) was low, the program's costs grew over time. Child ownership of the XOs meant that approximately one-third of the computer inventory left the program every year, as students either graduated from elementary school or moved out of the district. With the benefits minimal, the cost-benefit ratio was thus quite high. Local media derided the program as a "costly lesson" (Crowe, 2009). After the mayor and the city council leader who launched the program were both convicted and imprisoned for bribery, fraud, and misappropriation of funds (on other projects, including, in the City Council president's case, a previous program providing computers to children), the new mayor and city council eliminated further funding for the program. Few 1st-grade or transfer students received laptops this year, and the long-term status of the program is not promising. A National Science Foundation-funded project to train teachers is under way, but it is not likely to reverse the decline of the XO program, which the district superintendent is "tactically moving . . . to a subordinate position" (Birmingham News Editorial Board, 2010). Birmingham has learned its lesson the hard way. Just as music does not reside in the piano, teaching, learning, and knowledge do not reside in the computer.

The Birmingham program is in some ways an outlier; not many educational technology initiatives end up with their founders in prison. However, the underlying problem—of putting great faith in the power of technology to bring about improvement and insufficient attention to the surrounding factors needed to make technology successful—is unfortunately not uncommon. Rob Kling called this the *standard model* of technology implementation (Kling, 2000). From this perspective, technology is a tool to be passed out, implementations are one-shot, technological effects are direct and immediate, politics are irrelevant, social effects are benign, contexts are simple, knowledge and expertise are easily made explicit, and infrastructures are fully supportive. In fact, though, as Kling and others demonstrate through extensive research on technology deployments in schools, governments, and businesses, technology is more of a sociotechnical network than a tool, implementations are ongoing, effects are often indirect and involve multiple timescales, politics are central, social repercussions are unpredictable, contexts are highly complex, knowledge and expertise are inherently tacit or implicit, and much additional skill and work are needed to make infrastructures function appropriately (Kling, 1999, 2000; Kling & Lamb, 2001; Warschauer, 2003).

If we consider digital media not as a tool to be dropped into schools for bringing rapid change, but rather as part of a complex sociotechnical ecology for educational reform, important questions arise. What are the goals of reform? What is the particular contribution that digital media can make in helping to achieve these goals? What kinds of learning environments are best for that process? What kinds of curricula, pedagogy, and assessment should underlie a reform effort? And how can we develop a long-lasting sociotechnical infrastructure—from affordable tools, to effective leaders, to skilled and committed teachers—that can sustain successful reform?

Drawing on lessons from Littleton and other districts, this book examines these questions, addressing the *goals* of programs (Chapter 2); the hardware, software, and content *tools* they use (Chapter 3); the educational *designs* that frame them, including curriculum, pedagogy, and assessment (Chapter 5); and the sociotechnical infrastructure required to build and maintain learning *environments* (Chapter 6). To illuminate these discussions, we also look at four K–12 *exemplars* in depth (Chapter 4), each with a highly innovative curriculum deploying digital devices on a one-to-one basis.

We begin our discussion by critically evaluating the most frequently discussed reasons for integrating digital media in schools.

2

Goals

If you don't know where you're going, any road will take you there.
—George Harrison (2002)

Three main goals are put forward for using technology in education: (1) to improve academic achievement, (2) to facilitate new kinds of 21st-century learning, and (3) to promote educational and social equity. Each of these three is vitally important, but each is also often misunderstood. And when these goals are misconstrued and thus pursued incorrectly, we can actually end up further away from where want to get. The first step toward understanding how to integrate technology in education is to clarify what we hope to achieve and how. Let us start by critically examining each of these three goals in relationship to educational theory and practice.

ACADEMIC ACHIEVEMENT

The facts are stark. Among 8th-grade students in the United States, only 32% achieve proficient levels in reading, 34% in math, and 29% in science (National Assessment of Educational Progress, 2010). Nearly half of the remainder fail to reach even the basic level. Of students who enter the 9th grade in U.S. public schools, more than one-quarter fail to graduate 4 years later (Stilwell, 2010). In international comparisons among 30 developed countries, 15-year-olds in the United States rank 25th in math and 21st in science (Baldi et al., 2007).

Poor academic achievement tragically impacts life opportunities. Those who fail to graduate high school earn on average only $21,484 per year, compared to $57,181 for those with a bachelor's degree and $120,978 for those with a post-BA professional degree (U.S. Census Bureau, 2010). The neighborhoods and communities where those with limited education live are also impacted, as is the economic competitiveness of our nation.

Although current tests of academic achievement need improvement, as discussed later in this book, the message that these test results spell out—that too many of our students are failing to learn enough reading, writing, math, science, and history—needs to be taken seriously.

In recent years, the national agenda on academic achievement has been set by the No Child Left Behind Act, a bipartisan bill adopted in 2001. At the core of NCLB is the goal of improving education by insuring achievement of basic standards. The phrase "No Child Left Behind" refers to the Act's original goal that 100% of students will achieve basic proficiency in math and reading by 2014. Each year, schools, districts, and states are evaluated by the percentage of students who achieve basic proficiency on standardized tests in math and reading.

Although the goal of educating all students is admirable, the narrow focus on raising the percentage of students who achieve proficiency on standardized tests in two subject areas is problematic. Not only does this restricted focus crowd out other important educational objectives (such as preparing people to be good citizens and lifelong learners), but it also may be counterproductive for academic achievement as well. The enormous pressure placed on schools to raise test scores in the short term for a narrow band of students who are near basic proficiency can lead to educational decisions that limit long-term achievement for many students. These decisions include pushing students out of school who are unlikely to pass tests; failing to pay sufficient attention to students who are performing either too high or too low on tests and thus out of the targeted range for school improvement efforts; ignoring subjects such as science, social studies, and the arts that do not appear on elementary school standardized tests; or teaching reading and math in ways that are believed to boost test scores in the short term but may be ineffective in the long term (Rothstein, Jacobsen, & Wilder, 2008).

For example, literacy instruction in elementary schools focuses overwhelmingly on reading while downplaying writing, since the former is emphasized more on standardized tests, even though the latter is vital for long-term achievement across the curriculum. What's more, reading and language arts instruction tends to focus on discrete skills related to decoding, spelling, and grammar, all of which have value but which together represent a narrow subset of the skills and knowledge required for proficient reading (see, e.g., Paris, 2005). Test scores for students in lower primary grades have risen because of these approaches, but there have been few gains in the reading test scores of secondary students. That is not surprising, because unless students become more engaged in literacy through reading works of interest and discussing, analyzing, and writing about them, they are unlikely to transition well from *learning to read* (a basic skills process that should be largely completed by about 4th grade) to *reading to learn* (a vital lifelong skill; see discussion in Gee, 2004).

The educational technology correlate of focusing on discrete skills to raise test scores is the use of computers for drill and practice tutorials. A belief in the power of computer-based tutorials dates back to more than 50 years ago to when Skinner (1958) first proposed "teaching machines" (p. 969) as a more efficient and effective alternative to the progressive education approaches of Dewey. According to its advocates, computer-based tutorial learning helps students learn more, in a shorter time, with better retention, and at lower cost (see, e.g., Bork, 1985).

Tutorial learning fits well with the goals of No Child Left Behind since software can be selected that closely matches the content of grade-level standards and tests. This is in contrast, for example, to more open-ended technology-based instruction, such as for writing essays or carrying out project-based research, where students might venture into topics that are unlikely to be covered in this year's exams. Tutorial learning is widely used in schools. In a national survey, 50% of all teachers indicate that they sometimes or often deploy drill and practice programs and tutorials in instruction, and 69% indicate that their students sometimes or often use computers to learn or practice basic skills (Gray, Thomas, & Lewis, 2010b). The use of computer-based tutorials is especially prevalent in low-income schools, where 59% of teachers in low-income schools sometimes or often use drill and practice software, as opposed to 40% of teachers in high-income schools. The greater use of this software by teachers of low-income students likely corresponds both to the greater need for their students to develop basic skills as well as the intense pressure faced by schools in impoverished communities to increase academic performance.

However, research suggests that the effect of tutorial software on learning is minimal. In 2007, an experimental study was conducted on the impact of 16 commercial software products for tutorial learning in math and reading (Dynarski et al., 2007). Twelve of the 16 products had received or been nominated for awards by trade associations, media, teachers, or parents. A total of 439 teachers in 132 schools across the United States were randomly assigned to teach with or without the software. Those selected to use the software received specialized training in doing so. Technical difficulties using the products were mostly minor. Pre- and post-tests were administered to evaluate any changes in student achievement. Products were evaluated in four categories: 1st-grade reading, 4th-grade reading, 6th-grade math, and algebra. In all four of the categories, there were no significant differences in learning between the experimental classes that used the software and the control classes that did not.

Another recent study demonstrates why tutorial software is often unsuccessful and sometimes counterproductive. The Los Angeles Unified School District implemented a large-scale deployment of the Waterford Early Reading Program to try to raise the literacy skills of kindergarten and 1st-grade students (Llosa & Slayton, 2009). The software focuses on print concepts, phonological awareness, letter recognition, letter sounds, word recognition, and beginning reading comprehension. These are a subset of skills covered in the district's highly scripted reading text and curriculum known as *Open Court*. It was believed that students in low-achieving schools needed additional instructional time in reading and that they would benefit from an alternative instructional mode that was adaptable to their level and presumably more engaging than teacher-directed instruction. The district spent $64 million to purchase and sustain the program.

A rigorous 2-year evaluation comparing classes using and not using Waterford found no benefits from its use. Time spent utilizing the software tended to supplant other literacy instruction, and thus brought no new time on task. English language learners (ELLs) found the program confusing and uninteresting and, among ELLs, those with the least proficiency in English were most likely to be disengaged while using the software. Interestingly, similar results occurred when using the scripted *Open Court* textbooks in the district; of students who were disengaged with *Open Court*, most were ELLs and, among ELLs who were disengaged, most were at the lowest level of proficiencies. Those with the greatest reading difficulties in the district did not respond well to highly scripted instruction, whether it was provided via text or software.

If drill and practice software does not lead to academic achievement, what kinds of technology use do? Wenglinsky's (2005) detailed analysis of National Assessment of Educational Progress (NAEP) test score data answers this question. Based on the large size of the NAEP database, Wenglinsky was able to analyze the effect on student test scores of particular uses of technology, taking into account student and teacher background. In other words, he assessed the impact of a particular usage of technology for students of similar demographic backgrounds with teachers of similar background. Through this analysis, Wenglinsky found that use of computers for drill and practice (in mathematics) or for grammar and punctuation (in language arts) had negative correlations with student test scores. However, positive correlations were found for the use of simulations, data analysis, games, word processing, and writing in math, science, and reading test scores.

The inclusion of word processing and writing in Wenglinsky's findings is especially interesting, because at the time of his study, essay writing had not yet been included in the NAEP. Instead, Wenglinsky found positive results of using technology for writing on two other test scores, those for reading and science. This suggests that writing in schools is not only valuable for learning to compose, but also is valuable for learning reading and content material. This latter point is supported by Reeves (2002), who investigated what he calls *90/90/90 schools*—defined as highly successful schools with large numbers of low-income and minority students—and found that they universally place a high emphasis on informative writing. In Reeves's view, informational writing forces students to both think through their own ideas and make their thoughts visible for critique and feedback from others, thus leading to better comprehension of subject matter.

Wenglinsky's study and the others described above make evident that the most effective way to get from A to B is not always a straight line. Although drill and practice activities can be closely tied to state content standards, the use of such activities tends to be associated with lower test scores. Instead, it is the richer, more open-ended activities that are correlated with higher test scores, even when all other factors are held equal. Thus, if we wish to increase academic achievement, students should principally use the computer as *a tool to think with*—to carry out research, collect and analyze data, explore ideas through games and simulations, and write authentic texts—rather than as a tutor. These are exactly the kinds of cognitively challenging uses of technology frequently found in much project-based learning, which, if designed right, involves considering ideas and posing questions; gathering and analyzing information; creatively synthesizing information and solving problems; evaluating and revising results; and sharing, publishing, and/or acting on what was learned (Spires, Wiebe, Young, Hollebrands, & Lee, 2009).

This is not to suggest that that all drill and practice activities be banned from the classroom. Such activities may play a positive role when used in small supplementary ways. However, research to date should warn us away from viewing individual tutorials as the principal use of technology in instruction, and should instead guide us toward incorporating more creative simulations, games, writing, research, and project work, both to raise academic achievement and to promote 21st-century learning.

21ST-CENTURY LEARNING

Technology can be a lever to improve previously defined learning outcomes. However, its role in society and the economy can also make us rethink what learning is about. Throughout history, from the development of the printing press through more recent stages of industrialization, the nature of education has evolved in response to broader social, economic, and technological trends (for a review, see Warschauer, 1999). For example, literacy pedagogy in the agrarian era typically involved rote learning, oral recitation, copying, and imitation of correct speech and writing, with the curriculum principally based on the Bible, a narrow selection from Greek and Roman literature, and handwriting primers (de Castell & Luke, 1986). Just as visions of goals of literacy and learning changed from the agrarian era of the 19th century to the industrial era of the 20th century, so they must change again in the post-industrial 21st century.

Shaffer and Gee (2005) put forth perhaps the most compelling argument why the standardized education promoted by No Child Left Behind is outdated. As they point out, in a world in which the science and technology necessary for basic manufacturing has spread throughout the world, high-wage countries like the United States can no longer compete on the basis of making and selling commodities. A nation's competitive edge instead comes from how well it produces products, services, and technologies that are new, special, non-standard, and innovative. The value of such products does not reside primarily in the material or labor that goes into them, but rather in knowledge about "innovative design of new products, services, and technologies" and about "new forms of social interactions and relationships" (Shaffer & Gee, p. 4; see also Atkinson & Andes, 2009, and Augustine et al., 2010, for discouraging reports on U.S. competitiveness in innovation). Shaffer and Gee conclude that

> Our standards-driven curriculum, especially in urban schools, is not preparing children to be innovators at the highest technical levels—the levels that will pay off most in our modern, high-tech, science-driven, global economy. Inspired by the goal of leaving no child behind in basic skills, we are leaving all of our children, rich and poor, well behind in the new global competition for innovative work. Instead, we are busy preparing them for commodity jobs, most of which will be long gone by the time they finish school. (pp. 5–6)

Educational reform must address the kinds of skills and practices needed in the world our children will grow up in, and better use of technology in schools is essential for achieving this goal. However, just as with the goal of promoting academic achievement, precision in understanding the nature of this goal and how best to reach it is critical.

The most prominent organization addressing this topic is the Partnership for 21st Century Skills (P21), a national coalition of technology firms (e.g., Microsoft, Apple, Dell), publishers (e.g., Pearson, Houghton Mifflin, McGraw-Hill), game and entertainment companies (e.g., LEGO,

Disney), and educational groups (e.g., National Association of School Librarians, National Education Association). P21 calls for better aligning classroom environments with the requirements of 21st-century workplaces and communities by focusing on 21st-century skill outcomes—in life and career skills; learning and innovation skills; and information, media, and technology skills (see Figure 2.1)—in addition to core academic subjects (e.g., math, science, reading, language arts, history, geography) and themes (e.g., global awareness, environmental literacy; Partnership for 21st Century Skills, 2010).

The skills pointed to by P21 are of value. However, the P21 framework has come under criticism for overemphasizing skills that may be ephemeral, such as use of today's rapidly changing technology, over knowledge and understanding that should be more enduring (Common Core, 2010). A close reading of P21's materials suggests that these criticisms are exaggerated; P21 stresses that knowledge and skills must grow in tandem. However, the name of the group and the rhetoric of some of its advocates do seem to imply that skills can be learned independently of knowledge. Why such a separation is potentially dangerous can be seen from research in economics, cognitive science, and education.

Levy and Murnane (2004) refute the common wisdom that today's job market just needs skilled problem solvers without any particular expertise in content areas. Studying occupational change in the knowledge economy, the two economists found that job skill demand in areas of work that have been automated, such as *routine cognitive, routine manual,* and *nonroutine manual* work, has fallen in the digital era. Of greater interest is what they found about the two areas in which job demand is increasing. The first of these is what they call *expert thinking.* Although their use of this term has been interpreted by some to refer to generic thinking skills, Levy and Murnane mean something quite different. As they explain, expert thinking refers to the kind of advanced pattern recognition and problem solving that comes from deep knowledge and expertise in a particular domain. It is the expertise of a physician who can draw on both medical knowledge and clinical experience to make a challenging diagnosis, or of a mechanical engineer who draws on both his education and experience to identity a subtle structural problem. No set of generic thinking skills can substitute for the kinds of expertise these challenges demand.

Levy and Murnane call the second area "complex communication." Examples include "a biology teacher explaining how cells divide" and "an engineer describing why a new design for a DVD player is an advance over previous designs" (p. 48). Complex communicative ability relies heavily on specific content knowledge; the teacher, for example, cannot explain cell division well, whether directly to students or through development of

FIGURE 2.1. 21st-Century Skills

Learning and Innovation Skills

- Creativity and Innovation
- Critical Thinking and Problem Solving
- Communication and Collaboration

Information, Media and Technology Skills

- Information Literacy
- Media Literacy
- ICT (Information, Communications, and Technology) Literacy

Life and Career Skills

- Flexibility and Adaptability
- Initiative and Self-Direction
- Social and Cross-Cultural Skills
- Productivity and Accountability
- Leadership and Responsibility

Source: Partnership for 21st Century Skills (2010)

curricular material, without expertise in both biology and science pedagogy. It also involves writing well about specific content areas (National
Commission on Writing, 2004). Most of the highly skilled knowledge
workers who receive the greatest pay and prestige in today's economy,
such as professors, attorneys, executives, consultants, engineers, and systems analysts, need to write analytically and convincingly about complex
matters that demand content expertise as well as familiarity with scientific, legal, or other specific genres.

Cognitive science research confirms the close interaction between
knowledge and skill development. As nicely explained by Willingham
(2009), thinking—which he defines as combining information in new
ways—occurs when people draw information from either the environment or from long-term memory and process it in their working memory.
However, working memory is limited; most adults, for example, can only
remember five to nine digits given to them in a random sequence. For
working memory to proceed efficiently, it must draw on factual or procedural knowledge from long-term memory. That allows "chunking" to
occur, as new information is linked to old information, thus freeing up

more working memory capacity for further thinking. This, in turn, leads to the development of schema, or the linking of facts and information in mental structures that represent concepts and the relationship between them. The more relevant schema people have, the more information they can process and critically think about.

This is an important principle in reading theory, which recognizes that students' ability to understand and think critically about new passages is highly dependent on the background knowledge and schema they have on a topic. Willingham offers the example of a recent *Science* article entitled "Physical Model for the Decay and Preservation of Marine Organic Carbon." Only somebody with background knowledge on organic carbon can understand and critically evaluate such a paper. Although definitions of each of the article's words can be found on the Internet, those lacking sufficient background knowledge on the topic would quickly find their working memory overwhelmed in trying to understand, let alone critically think about, the content of this paper, the online availability of definitions notwithstanding.

Background knowledge is not only important for achieving basic understanding, but also for deploying advanced skills, such as problem solving. When faced with a problem, people usually engage in long-term memory retrieval and search for a solution based on existing knowledge and experience. The less existing knowledge they have on a topic, the more difficult it is for them to solve complex new problems in the domain. As Glaser (1984) concluded from his seminar paper in this area, "the problem-solving difficulty of novices can be attributed, to a large extent, to the inadequacies of their knowledge bases, and not to . . . the inability to use problem-solving heuristics. Novices show effective heuristics" (p. 99). Glaser explains that learning and reasoning skills develop not as abstract mechanisms, but rather "as the content and concepts of a knowledge domain are attained in learning situations" (p. 99).

An obvious example is seen in the field of chess, always a favorite among cognitive scientists. Grandmasters can think critically about chess moves and solve chess problems not because they have some advanced critical thinking ability honed through generic learning processes, but rather because they have patterns imbedded in their mind from years of playing and studying chess. Similarly, students can think more critically about how a particular war started or why a mathematical proof is illogical if they have domain knowledge in an area. Finally, the effects of lack of background knowledge can be compounding and accumulative, since how much you already know affects the rate of new knowledge acquisition. In this case, as Willingham notes, the rich get richer.

Examples from Schools

Most people involved in educational practice, policy, or research would agree that both knowledge and 21st-century skills are of value in instruction. However, research in schools suggests that much technology-oriented instruction fails to achieve a good balance. On the one hand, tutorial-based software such as that discussed previously usually does little to foster communication, collaboration, autonomous learning, and other 21st-century skills. On the other hand, some technology-oriented instruction purportedly offered in support of 21st-century learning de-emphasizes knowledge. For example, the use of PowerPoint for student presentations is almost ubiquitous in U.S. schools, with students sometimes assessed on the variety of animations or colors they include rather than the content or communicative value of their presentation (Warschauer, Knobel, & Stone, 2004). Similarly, students are sometimes praised for creating Internet-based projects, even if the content represents little more than cutting and pasting from the first sites they find (Warschauer, 2006). Our research suggests that an emphasis on soft skills of communication and collaboration *instead of* rather than *in addition to* content knowledge is more likely to occur in low-income communities. An example of this is seen in the following study I did of two schools in Hawaii, both with a reputation of excellence in uses of technology, but with different contexts and approaches to the integration of knowledge and skill (Warschauer, 2000).

Kaunani (the names of both schools are pseudonyms) is one of the most expensive private schools in Hawaii and one of the top-ranked college preparatory schools in the United States. Approximately 97% of its students go on directly to 4-year colleges and universities, with many enrolling in elite private colleges on the U.S. mainland. Leina, in contrast, is a public school in an impoverished community, with most students qualifying for free or reduced-cost lunch programs and some living in homeless encampments on nearby beaches. At the time of my study, only 11% of Leina seniors reported that they planned to enter directly into a 4-year college or university. Both Kaunani and Leina had reputations for excellent use of technology. However, observations, interviews, and document analysis revealed a sharp difference in approach. Simply put, whereas Kaunani taught 21st-century skills in the context of advanced domain knowledge, Leina often focused on 21st-century skills instead of advanced domain knowledge.

For example, both schools had specialized science programs, specifically a Marine Science program at Leina and an Advanced Placement biology program at Kaunani. Although they were not equivalent courses—

neither one existed at the other school—each was considered among the best science courses that the school had to offer. The Biology students at Kaunani were being apprenticed as junior scientists. They performed the kind of experiments that scientists might perform. And they used computers as tools in this process. Specifically, they used special handheld devices to probe the temperature, acidity, absorption spectra, and other features of plant life in the classroom and in nearby ponds. They then downloaded data from these devices to personal computers, where special software allowed them to graph, compare, and interpret the data. The teacher of the course teamed up with a mathematics instructor, so his students could learn to better make use of calculus in their data analysis. The teacher explained to me his approach to using technology in the course:

> We've been working over the years on our biology program,
> particularly our Advanced Biology program, to give students the
> type of experience that they need to prepare them for college
> work. . . . I had been a research scientist at Berkeley and Stanford
> as a graduate student. So I have a very strong background in
> research, which I loved. And I try to share that love of research
> with my students. And since I was pretty much lab-oriented and
> biochemistry-oriented I did what I knew and tried to implement
> those kinds of experiments. And it became obvious over the last
> 10 years, the computers were becoming one of the most important
> scientific tools available. And so we wanted to implement the
> computers into the program. We had cooperation from the parent/
> faculty association and the administration. And they funded our
> computer program. And we realized that this was an important
> scientific direction for our students to go.

In contrast, the Marine Science program at Leina, while engaging, motivating, and interesting to the students, had much less to do with scientific inquiry or disciplinary knowledge. The students grew seaweed in special outdoor ponds. They traveled on a boat trip around Oahu. And they used computers to collaboratively produce a regular newsletter about their personal experiences. The newsletter included articles describing the students' boat voyage, their journals, and the people they met. For team teaching, the instructor teamed up with a business teacher, so her students could learn to better market their seaweed. The instructor put a great deal of time and effort getting her students to learn to cooperate together, especially as it involved computer work. The monthly newsletter the students produced was done almost entirely through their own work, with students working in teams to write articles, edit one another's work, and select graphics. The newsletter project could be considered a model for writing across the curriculum, but it wasn't particularly related to science. In fact, the teacher gave the students full credit for completing the computer requirements of her class, even if they only typed up something for another one of their classes, since her real goal, as she explained to me, was for her students to become computer-literate.

Nor were some of her other activities oriented toward mastery of science. For example, students got together once a week to read stories from an inspirational book and to write their own inspirational stories, perhaps a valuable activity for writing and personal growth, but unrelated to science. She explained to me how her value-based cooperative learning was tied, in her eyes, to the vocational needs of the students.

> I looked at these kids and I said, how many of them are going into a science-related field? Out of 50, it's lucky if 3 or 4 of them would go into something science-related. So I said, this is really not acceptable. And that's where I changed my focus. As far as I'm concerned, they don't have to learn the science or learn the material, as long as they're doing these projects. But my focus is on them being respectful, responsible, and seekers of information. And I said, then I don't care what you do, whether you go out and be a trash (man) or dig ditches or if you go into a community college.

The Marine Science teacher justified her approach based on the stated needs of local employers. As she explained to me,

> The really interesting thing is about 2 or 3 years ago this whole school-to-work thing came out. And they went to big companies, and they asked these employers, they said, when our students graduate from high school what do you want them to know? And the employers all came up and said, We don't care what they studied, we want a student who's respectful, who's responsible, who can work together with other people and want to learn, we can train them. We don't care. We don't need them to be honors students and all that. We can train them on the job. Give us kids who know how to be respectful, responsible team players. And so it's right in line with what we've been doing and I feel really good about that . . . 'cause this is what employers want.

The teacher is probably correct in pointing out what many employers want. However, there is a bifurcation of the 21st-century job market. In an information-based economy, even entry-level office jobs require many things labeled as 21st-century skills, such as being able to make use of new technology to communicate and collaborate. However, the greatest power, pay, and influence are reserved for those who have more than these basic skills, specifically those who also can carry out expert thinking and complex communication in particular domains.

The context in these two schools is, of course, not comparable. The science teacher at Leina may have had a good read on the prospects of students in her program and was perhaps doing as much as she could to help them reach achievable goals. On a broader level, though, I would suggest that Kaunani and Leina are illustrative of differences between one approach that emphasizes 21st-century skills in the service of mastering knowledge, and one that emphasizes 21st-century skills in their own right. Looking at the big picture, it is important for schools to do the former as much as possible, rather than just the latter.

Adaptive Expertise

A helpful model for considering the relationship between, on the one hand, knowledge and skill in particular domain areas, and, on the other hand, 21st-century skills of inquiry and innovation, is provided by Bransford and colleagues (Bransford et al., 2009). According to their model (see Figure 2.2), the worst outcome occurs if inquiry and innovation are emphasized without the development of specific skills and knowledge. That tends to result in *frustrated novices*, who become neither expert nor innovative because they simply don't know enough to get started in an area. A focus on specific skills and knowledge, such as algorithms for solving math problems, is somewhat better, because it can result in *routine experts* on particular topics. Far best, though, is a combination of specific skills and knowledge with inquiry and innovation. That approach enables people to constantly stretch their knowledge so they can apply it in a range of different areas and disciplines, and eventually become what Bransford and his colleagues call *adaptive experts*.

According to Bransford, adaptive experts can not only perform procedural skills efficiently, but also better understand the meaning and nature of their object. They can verbalize the principles underlying their skills, judge conventional and unconventional versions of skills as appropriate, and modify or invent skills according to local constraints. By avoiding the tendency to overapply previously efficient schemas, they are thus better prepared to learn in new situations (Hatano & Oura, 2003). Bransford and colleagues provide the example of Dr. Steven Phillips, a heart transplant surgeon who developed artificial hearts, valves, and other vital devices, and who learned to balance efficiency and innovation, the former in his

FIGURE 2.2. Dimensions of Adaptive Expertise

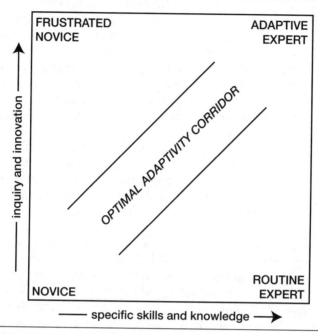

Source: Bransford, J., Mosborg, S., Copland, M. A., Honig, M. A., Nelson, H. G., Gawel, D. et al. (2009)

surgery and the latter in his development and perfection of new devices and surgical techniques. They suggest that this kind of adaptive expertise is needed today more than ever, since the rapidly developing economy will require people to either change jobs with accelerated frequency, or, if they stay on the same job, respond innovatively to new environments and situations.

This model is very helpful for thinking about improving K–12 education. As Bransford and colleagues explain,

> For educators, this model becomes especially useful when we ask how we can move people along both of its dimensions, because movement along one dimension alone is unlikely to support the development of adaptive expertise. Training dedicated to high efficiency can overly constrain transfer and restrict it primarily to highly similar situations (e.g., National Research Council, 2000). By the same token, opportunities to develop general, content-free skills of critical thinking or problem solving appear to provide a set of flexible but *weak methods* that are too inefficient for the large problem spaces found in many real-world tasks. (Newell & Simon, 1972, cited in Bransford et al., 2009, p. 830)

These arguments suggest that people will benefit most from learning opportunities that balance the two dimensions . . . and remain within the *optimal adaptability corridor*. For example, children who receive nothing but efficiency-oriented computation training in mathematics may well become efficient, but this kind of experience can lead to limited conceptual understanding, which hampers flexibility when they face new problems (Martin & Schwartz, 2005; National Research Council, 2000). Balanced instruction in mathematics, for example, includes opportunities for people to learn with understanding—in part by posing and testing their own mathematical conjectures. They can then be exposed to solutions developed over the centuries, plus be provided with multiple efficiency-building experiences. Instruction that *balances* efficiency and innovation seems optimal and should include opportunities to experiment with ideas and, in the process, experience the need to change them and develop the proficiency to make them work (Schwartz & Bransford, 1998; Schwartz & Martin, 2004).

This model of adaptive expertise helps illustrate why project-based learning is potentially valuable. If designed well, project-based learning helps students pose and test their own conjectures, experiment with ideas, experience the need to change them, and develop the proficiency to make them work. However, their model also suggests that problem-based learning works best when infused with strong content instruction (which can be provided either before, during, or after the periods of inquiry and project work), since, over time, lack of sufficient content instruction will leave people unprepared to tackle challenging real-world tasks. This can especially occur with learners who, due to socioeconomic status, language background, or other factors, are already struggling in school—which brings us to our next topic: educational equity.

EDUCATIONAL EQUITY

Among developed countries, the United States is one of the most stratified in educational achievement and attainment. Students from the top income quartile in the United States are 8.3 times more likely than those in the bottom income quartile to have completed a BA degree (Rosenstone, 2005). African-American and Latino youth perform perilously low on achievement tests (see Table 2.1), and nearly half fail to graduate from high school (Orfield, Losen, Wald, & Swanson, 2004). Disaggregated by race and comparing internationally, White students in the United States would rank second out of 29 countries around the world in reading, whereas Black and Hispanic students would rank 26th (Tienken, 2010).

TABLE 2.1. Percent of 8th-Grade Students Scoring at or Above Proficient Level, 2009

	Black	Hispanic	White	Asian
Math	12	17	44	54
Reading	14	17	41	45

Addressing this severe educational inequality is a critical challenge in the United States.

Educational and social equity are closely connected to issues of technology access, use, and mastery. Computer and Internet use is required by the majority of the fastest-growing occupations (listed at Bureau of Labor Statistics, 2008), and sophisticated use is required by the aforementioned knowledge workers who have the greatest economic and social opportunities. Manuel Castells (1998), whose three-volume work analyzed the new knowledge economy and the role of digital media in it, concluded that "information technology, and the ability to use it and adapt it, is the critical factor in generating and accessing wealth, power, and knowledge in our time" (p. 98).

Although technology can be a lever to promote educational equity, how to use it for that purpose is far from straightforward, as will be seen from a review of research on issues of technology access, use, and outcomes among U.S. youth.

Home and Community Access

Although there are still substantial differences in access to digital media at home by race and ethnicity in the United States (for a review, see Warschauer & Matuchniak, 2010), these differences are narrower among households that have children. A national survey of youth conducted in 2008–2009 by the Kaiser Family Foundation (KFF) found that among 8- to 18-year-olds, 94% of Whites, 89% of Blacks, and 92% of Hispanics have computers at home (Rideout, Foehr, & Roberts, 2010). Differences in access to the Internet by parental education are a bit larger, with 91% of children whose parents graduated from college reporting Internet access at home compared to 74% of children whose parents never went to college.

Access to technology is not a binary division between information haves and have-nots; rather, there are differing degrees and types of access depending on the type and amount of equipment at home and speed of Internet access (see discussion in Warschauer, 2003). Social factors are likely even more important than technical factors in shaping access.

With computer mastery depending heavily on social support, both from peers (see, e.g., Margolis, Estrella, Goode, Holme, & Nao, 2008) and family members (see, e.g., Barron, Martin, Takeuchi, & Fithian, 2009), many low-income or immigrant youth will have few friends or relatives who are sophisticated users of digital media. Conditions in the household and neighborhood, such as relatively few computers, lesser degrees of broadband Internet access, fewer people with a college education, and fewer English speakers, are likely to shape the kinds of experience youths have with digital media and the extent to which these experiences foster learning.

The influence of family members on children's experience with technology and on the relationship of technology use to other proficiencies is illustrated by a study in Philadelphia that examined children's use of city libraries before and after the introduction of computers (Neuman & Celano, 2006). The study found that after the libraries got computers, children in low-income communities, who typically received little parent mentoring in libraries, spent considerable time either waiting for computers to be free or playing computer-based games with little textual content. Technology thus displaced reading for these children. In contrast, parents in middle-income communities "carefully orchestrated children's activities on the computer, much as they did with books" (p. 193). Children in those communities thus spent more time on print-based computer applications, averaging 11 lines of print per application compared to 3.9 lines of print for the children in low-income communities. As a result, children in middle-income communities doubled the amount of time spent on reading following the introduction of technology, and the gap in print access between low- and high-income youth increased.

School Access

There have been steady gains in equitable access to technology in schools, but, once again, small gaps persist. A national survey conducted in fall 2008 found that the ratio of instructional computers with Internet access per student in schools that had less than 6% minority students was 2.8 (Gray et al., 2010a). In schools that had 50% or greater minority student enrollment, the ratio was 3.2.

As in home environments, sociotechnical factors support or constrain the use of computers and the Internet in schools, often in ways that heighten educational inequity. A comparative study of school technology use in high- and low-socioeconomic (SES) communities found that the low-SES neighborhood schools tended to have less stable teaching staff, administrative staff, and technology support staff, which made planning for technology use more difficult (Warschauer et al., 2004). As the study reported, the high-SES schools "tended to invest more in professional development, hiring full-time technical support staff and developing lines of communication among teachers, office staff, media specialists, technical staff, and administration that promoted robust digital networks." This, in turn, "encouraged more widespread teacher use of new technologies." In comparison, "the low-SES schools had achieved less success in creating the kinds of support networks that made technology workable" (p. 581). Since teachers in low-SES schools were less confident that the equipment they signed up for would actually work, and that if it didn't work, they would have available timely technical support, they were more reluctant to rely on technology in their lesson plans.

In addition, even when teachers in low-SES schools had confidence in the hardware and software they were using, the sheer complexity of their instructional environments made it more difficult to use technology well. Challenges they faced included larger numbers of English language learners and at-risk students, larger numbers of students with limited computer experience, and greater pressure to increase test scores and adhere to policy mandates.

Home and Community Use

Although Black and Hispanic youths have less access to computers and the Internet than White youths both at home and at school, they tend to spend more time online than White youth in a typical day. According to the KFF's survey of 8- to 18-year-olds, the average amount of time spent using a computer on a typical day is 1 hour, 24 minutes for Blacks; 1 hour, 49 minutes for Hispanics; and 1 hour, 17 minutes for Whites. This is consistent with other media trends in the United States, with Black and Hispanic youth also spending more time per day than White youth watching TV, listening to music, playing video games, and watching movies, and with these gaps increasing over the years (Rideout et al., 2010). In addition, Black and Hispanic teens make many more cell phone calls than White teens per month, and are much more likely to use cell phones to go online (Lenhart, Ling, Campbell, & Purcell, 2010). The only media that White youth spend more time with per day than Black or Hispanic youth is print media (Rideout et al., 2010).

A recent report, based on interviews and observations with hundreds of middle school– and high school–aged youth, provides an in-depth view of how youth use digital media outside of school (Ito et al., 2009). Ito and her colleagues identified two primary categories of online practices, which they label *friendship-driven* and *interest-driven*. Friendship-driven practices essentially involve hanging out with their peers online and either take the place of or complement other forms of youth socializing, such as gathering at the mall. The principal tools for hanging out are social network sites (specifically MySpace and Facebook), instant messaging, and computer and video games. Typical friendship-driven activities include chatting or flirting; uploading, downloading, or discussing music, images, and video; updating profiles and writing on friends' walls; and playing or discussing games. Almost all youth participate in these friendship activities, and minority youth do so the most. For example, Blacks and Hispanics age 8 to 18 spend more time per day on social network sites than do White youth (Rideout et al., 2010), and Black and Hispanics age 12 and above are far more likely than Whites to use Twitter (Smith & Rainie, 2010; Webster, 2010).

Most youth do not move beyond friendship-driven activities, but the more creative and adventurous explore interest-driven genres. As with friendship-driven activities, interest-driven activities typically involve communicating, game playing, and sharing of media. But in interest-driven genres, it is the specialized activity, interest, or niche identity that is the driving motivation, rather than merely socializing with local peers. This results in a much deeper and more sophisticated engagement with new media, and also brings participants into communication and collaboration with people of diverse ages and backgrounds around the world, rather than principally with their own local peers. The Digital Youth Project identified two stages of interest-driven participation, which they label *messing around* and *geeking out*. Messing around involves early exploration of personal interests, wherein young people "begin to take an interest in and focus on the workings and content of the technology and media themselves, tinkering, exploring, and extending their understanding" (Ito et al., 2008, p. 20). Activities in this regard include searching for information online and experimenting with digital media production or more complex forms of gaming. Geeking out is the next stage, and involves "an intense commitment to or engagement with media or technology, often one particular media property, genre, or type of technology" and "learning to navigate esoteric domains of knowledge and practice and participating in communities that traffic in these forms of expertise" (Ito et al., 2008, p. 28). Examples of geeking out include creation and sharing of animated films that use computer game engines and footage (machinima); posting and critiquing of creative writing related to popular culture (fan fiction); development and publishing of videos based on clips from anime series that are set to songs (anime music videos); writing and distribution of subtitles of foreign films or television programs, especially anime, within hours after the films or programs are released (fansubbing); and creation and posting of short dramatic or humorous films on YouTube (video production).

Scholars such as Gee (2003, 2004) and Jenkins (2009) persuasively argue that youth's participation in new media provides vital learning experiences. However, Gee and Jenkins principally focus on youth who are engaged in interest-driven activities, and especially those who "geek out." Yet, the Ito study reports that only a small minority of youth move on to this geeking out stage, and also makes evident that access to additional technological and social resources, beyond a simple computer and Internet account, is critical in determining who moves on to these more sophisticated forms of media participation. Given the nature of geeking out activities, technological resources presumably include broadband access, relatively new computers with graphics and multimedia capacity, digital production software, and equipment such as digital cameras and camcorders. Social resources include a community that values and enables the sharing of media knowledge and interests, which can be found among family, friends, or interest groups, or in organized programs at computer clubs and youth media centers.

Ito's study does not attempt to identify those who typically move on to the geeking out stage and those who do not, but other studies address this issue. A compelling account is provided by Attewell and Winston (2003), who spent several months observing and interviewing two groups of computer users at home and school. The first group consisted of African American and Latino children age 11 to 14 who attended public middle school; most came from poor and working-class families, and all scored below grade level in reading. The second group consisted of schoolchildren from more affluent families who attended private schools.

The wealthier youths studied by Attewell and Winston frequently engaged in interest-driven activities. For example, a White 4th-grade private school student named Zeke was a "political junky at ten years old" (p. 124). He spent his online time reading up on the presidential inauguration, downloading video clips of politicians, and reading candidates' speeches. He then collaborated with other students to launch and participate in an election for class president, an unofficial position that was not sanctioned by the teachers at the school. To organize the election, Zeke found a free Website that allowed visitors to construct quizzes and modified it to develop an online voting system. With the cooperation of his rival for office, he told each child in his class to visit the Web page for the voting system, both to read the campaign speeches that he and his opponent posted and eventually to vote.

The low-SES group also pursued their interests, but in very different ways. Typical was Kadesha, a 13-year-old African American girl. Kadesha and her friends spent much of their online time checking out rappers and wrestlers (whom they referred to as their "husbands"), downloading their pictures as screensavers and pasting images into reports (p. 117). They also went cyber–window shopping together, checking out everything from hot new sneakers to skateboards to Barbie dolls. The authors explained how Kadesha's ability to exploit the Internet was greatly restricted by her limited reading and writing skills:

> As image after image flashes by, . . . it becomes noticeable how rarely, how lightly, Kadesha settles on printed text. Like many of her friends, she reads far below grade level. So she energetically pursues images and sounds on the Web, but foregoes even news of her love interest if that requires her to read. (p. 117)

Of course, working with images and sounds can be an important part of geeking out, but Attewell and Winston's description makes clear that, in the case of Kadesha and many of her friends, engagement with multimedia was at the most basic level.

These qualitative findings of discrepancies are supported by national population survey data analyzed by DeBell and Chapman (2006). They found that, among children in grades pre-K to 12 who used a computer at home, Whites were more likely than Blacks or Hispanics to use word processing, e-mail, multimedia, and spreadsheets or databases. These applications were also more widely used by children who lived in high-income families, those with well-educated parents, and those with English-speaking parents, as compared to children from low-income families or whose parents did not graduate high school or did not speak English. Further evidence comes from a recent study comparing creative computing participation by youth in a high-SES California community and in a nearby low-SES community. Students in the high-SES community had greater home access to diverse digital tools (including computers, the Internet, printers, scanners, handheld devices, digital cameras, and video cameras) and were much more likely to have both depth and breadth of experience in digital media production (Barron, Walter, Martin, & Schatz, 2010).

School Use

The two widest U.S. studies (Becker, 2000b; Wenglinsky, 1998) on use of technology in schools by demographic groups were conducted in the 1990s. Both showed sharp disparities by race and SES in how new technologies were deployed for education.

Wenglinsky (1998) analyzed data from the 1996 National Assessment of Educational Progress (NAEP) to describe technology use patterns of 6,627 4th-graders and 7,146 8th-graders across the United States. Of all racial groups, African Americans were more likely to use computers at least once a week for mathematics at both the 4th-grade and 8th-grade level, likely due to the frequent use of remedial computer-based drills in math.

Wenglinsky divided up computer use into two broad categories. The first involved applying concepts or developing simulations to use them, activities that are both thought of as teaching higher-order skills. The second involved drill and practice activities, which by nature focus on lower-order skills. The study found that substantial differences by race/ethnicity, school lunch eligibility, and/or type of school exist with regard to whether students reported their teachers primarily using these activities. Most notably, more than three times as many Asian students as Black students reported their teachers as primarily using simulations and applications in 8th-grade mathematics instruction, whereas only about half as many Asians as Blacks reported their teachers primarily using drill and practice.

In the second national study, Becker surveyed a representative sample of 4,000 teachers across the United States. His study confirmed the differences found by Wenglinsky, and found that they applied more generally rather than just in mathematics (Becker, 2000b; Cohen & Miyake, 1986). Specifically, he found that teachers in low-SES schools were more likely to use computers for remediation and mastery of discrete skills, whereas teachers in high-SES schools were more likely to use computers for innovative and constructivist activities involving written expression, analysis of information, and public presentation.

Academic Outcomes

Evidence is mixed as to whether home access to computers brings positive academic outcomes (see discussion in Warschauer & Matuchniak, 2010), but there is broad agreement that any benefits gained are strongly mediated by student SES. For example, using the National Longitudinal Youth Survey (NLYS88), Attewell and Battle (1999) found that among families with home computers, and controlling for all other possible variables, children from high-SES families compared to low-SES families receive more than four and a half times the benefit in increased math scores and more than two and a half times the benefit in increased reading scores. Their study also found that White students received significantly greater benefit from home computer use on math and reading outcomes than did Black or Hispanic students. Although their data provide no firm evidence as to why these differences exist, they speculate that it may be due to the *social envelope* (Giacquinta, Bauer, & Levin, 1993) that surrounds children's home use of computers and includes technology resources (e.g., educational software) and social resources (scaffolding, modeling, and support from parents). They conclude that "Home computing may generate another 'Sesame Street effect' whereby an innovation that held great promise for poorer children to catch up educationally . . . is in practice increasing the educational gap between affluent and poor . . . even among those with access to the technology" (Attewell & Battle, 1999, p. 1).

Attewell and Battle's study is based on data that are some 20 years old, and the amount of home computers and the ways they are used have expanded dramatically during this time. However, a recent paper by three Duke economists reports similar results from a study in North Carolina, with race and SES strongly mediating the effect on academic achievement of home computer and Internet access (Vigdor & Ladd, 2010). The Duke findings are even more disheartening, as the study indicates an overall negative effect on math and reading test scores for low-SES and African-American students with computer and Internet access, apparently because "unproductive computer use is crowding out schoolwork of all kinds" (p. 28).

Studies of academic outcomes from school use of technology are mixed (Kulik, 2003). Many studies are based on very small sample sizes and take place in schools or classrooms where individual educators are highly expert in particular uses of technology, and thus these studies may not be generalizable to other contexts. However, larger studies, such as the one carried out by Wenglinsky (2005) that was discussed earlier, suggest that low-SES students typically benefit less from using technology at school than do high-SES students, apparently in part because of the more limited range of ways that they use computers in education. Exceptions to this are possible, though, as seen in some of our own recent research discussed later in this book.

Promoting Educational Equity with Technology

Given this context, how can technology best be deployed in education to ensure the most equitable academic, social, and economic outcomes? The traditional framework for considering this has been the notion of a *digital divide*. Since ethnic minorities and the poor had lesser access to digital media at home, this digital divide could be bridged by providing access to computers and the Internet either at home or at school, so the thinking went. Over time, the concept of easing a digital divide worked its way into numerous educational technology policy documents (Culp, Honey, & Mandinach, 2005).

While the sentiment is right, the concept itself is confusing and can divert attention from the best solutions. Its name and common usage emphasize the importance of the physical presence of computers and connectivity instead of other factors that allow people to use technology for meaningful ends. The term can thus suggest that the problem is primarily technological, whereas, as seen from the discussion above, differences in access to computers and connectivity have narrowed substantially, and African-American or Hispanic youth actually spend more time using digital media in a day than do White youth. The problems are thus not principally digital, but rather economic, social, and educational. The concept of a digital divide thus provides a poor roadmap for using technology to promote educational equity as Rob Kling, former director of the Center for Social Informatics at Indiana University, explained:

> [The] big problem with "the digital divide" framing is that it tends to connote "digital solutions," i.e., computers and telecommunications, without engaging the important set of complementary resources and complex interventions to support social inclusion, of which informational technology applications may be enabling elements, but are certainly insufficient when simply added to the status quo mix of resources and relationships. (Warschauer, 2003, pp. 7–8)

This is not just an academic point. The Birmingham program above perfectly illustrates the problems a governmental entity encounters when it seeks to overcome a digital divide through the provision of hardware or software without engaging in the broader educational reform and infrastructure development required for the hardware and software to be used effectively.

Technology *can* play a vital role in promoting educational and social equity, if deployed as part of well-designed educational interventions. Providing equipment is an important part of this effort, but a small part. Most important is to design an educational intervention that helps all students achieve excellence and that, in particular, provides the instruction, scaffolding, and support to especially help those at risk. This takes a thoughtful and intentional effort, since merely providing technological resources will likely amplify divides rather than narrow them, as those who begin with more skills and privilege will be able to leverage them for even greater success. However, there are strategies for using technology to heighten the performance of at-risk students, as will be seen in the remainder of this book. Indeed, all four of the programs that we highlight in Chapter 4 do an outstanding job of using technology to promote educational equity. Before reviewing them, let us first examine the kind of instructional environments and resources that these and other schools provide toward those ends.

3

Tools

Technology must be like oxygen: ubiquitous, necessary, and invisible.

—Chris Lehmann (2010)

If our goals for education are academic achievement, 21st-century learning, and educational equity, then what are the hardware, software, and digital content tools we need to succeed? Research both in and out of schools suggests that digital media help enable four critical functions of learning, each of which contributes to the earlier-discussed goals of academic achievement, 21st-century learning, and educational equity. I collectively call these the four Cs: content, community, construction, and composition.

To understand how each of these four functions aids learning, it is helpful to take another look at out-of-school learning, and particularly the advanced learning experiences of those who are able to "geek out" with new technologies in home environments (see examples in Gee, 2003, and in Ito et al., 2009). First, highly successful out-of-school learners use computers and the Internet to access individualized, differentiated, rich, and interactive *content* on topics they want to learn about. They find this through Websites, discussion forums, multiplayer games, mobile applications (apps), and other online resources. Second, they learn about this content with the support of a *community*, as peers and mentors play, discuss, and collaborate with them, both online and offline. Over time, they begin engaging in *construction* of meaningful public entities or artifacts, from imagery to avatars to videos, and their constructions become steadily more sophisticated over time as they continually interact with content and the community. Finally, in most of these situations, they are also engaged in extensive writing or *composition*, on journals, blogs, wikis, fan fiction networks, and other sites.

Each of these four Cs also finds resonance with educational theory and research. The best schools are known for providing students the most diverse, rich, and differentiated educational content—for example, through well-equipped libraries (see, e.g., McQuillan, 1998). When students take content and use it to construct and reconstruct things, they are pushed to confront and overcome limitations in their own thinking and mental models and to use knowledge they are gaining in increasingly innovative ways (Papert, 1993). Communication and support from others are vital for this process as it helps them advance through what Vygotsky (1978) calls a *zone of proximal development*, that is, the distance between what they can achieve when assisted by others and what they can achieve by themselves, and progress from being a peripheral to a more central member of a community of practice (Lave & Wenger, 1991). Finally, through extensive writing, they further sharpen their ideas (Black, 2008) while developing a vital skill for 21st-century life (National Commission on Writing, 2004).

All of these functions can be carried out without computers, and top-notch schools have long worked to provide students rich individualized content, social support for learning from peers and mentors, and opportunities to construct or compose meaningful products. However, each of these functions can be carried out much more effectively with the use of digital media, which can provide a vast amount of interactive content; put people in touch with others across the classroom or world; provide a means for advanced design and construction in the arts, engineering, and other fields; and help learners write, receive feedback, revise, and publish their work for authentic audiences.

Finally, although technology can facilitate learning in all these ways, it can also hinder learning. Computer breakdowns, network problems, dead batteries, or the need to learn new computer functions can disrupt class time. The sheer physicality of computers—their size on desks or their weight in backpacks—can interfere. Hardware, software, and maintenance can cost so much money that other important educational goals are crowded out. The best technologies are thus the ones that can be introduced with the least disruption in terms of cost, size, maintenance, ease of use, and learning curve.

GOING ONE-TO-ONE

One-to-one environments, where all students have access to their own computer or digital device, are the best for enabling content access, community building, construction, and composition—and, if implemented well, can also provide the most seamless technological solution. Research suggests that when students access computers on a shared or scheduled basis, they spend a disproportionate amount of time mastering hardware and software basics, rather than deploying the technology for broader learning ends (Warschauer et al., 2004). Lessons have to be rearranged to fit with the availability of technology, rather than the technology being picked up as necessary to support learning, as occurs when students have consistent day-to-day access to individual devices (Warschauer, 2006).

Educational leaders recognize the benefits of one-to-one programs. A national survey conducted in 2007 found that school districts in the United States are very satisfied with their one-to-one laptop programs, and the main impediment to the growth of such programs is their cost (Greaves & Hayes, 2008). However, the costs of equipment are continuing to decline, and the potential benefits are rising due to improvements in hardware and software, the creation of low-cost digital content, the steady migration of educational assessment to digital realms, and the gradual increase in technological skill among teachers and students.

The laptop has been the prototypical device to provide one-to-one access in schools. It remains a compelling choice due to its combination of power and portability. However, the device market is evolving, with a convergence between computer and mobile hardware that provides new options. We consider five important technologies that have contributed to this convergence—netbooks, open source software, social media, cloud computing, and media tablets—and the affordances they offer for education.

NETBOOKS

In recent years, a "good enough revolution" (Capps, 2009) has occurred in the technology marketplace. Digital services and products have seized market share, not because they are of higher quality, but because they are smaller, cheaper, and easier to use. People use Skype to make calls and Hulu to watch shows in spite of inferior audio and video compared to telephones and televisions because they are cheap and convenient. The prototypical example of a good enough product was the Flip video camera, which produced recordings of lower quality than other digital camcorders, but became successful due to its light weight, low cost, and convenience of use, until the Flip itself was made superfluous by smartphones.

The emergence of netbooks represents another example of "good enough." Netbooks have less powerful processors and fewer features than a typical laptop, but at a smaller size (typically with 7- to 12-inch displays), lower weight (typically under 3 pounds), lower cost, and with longer battery life (up to 8 hours with a 6-cell battery). The netbook industry traces back to the development of the OLPC's small XO computer, which cost a fraction of the price of typical laptops when it was released. Intel soon created a competing educational netbook called the Classmate PC. In 2007, first Asus and then a whole host of other computer companies began selling mass-market netbooks, and by 2010 netbooks had taken over a healthy chunk of the laptop market in the United States and around the world. Netbooks have also become the computer of choice for most recently launched one-to-one programs, including national programs in Uruguay (with the XO) and Portugal (with the Classmate PC), and a statewide program in New South Wales, Australia (with Lenovo). In the United States, schools are using a wide range of netbooks in one-to-one programs, including the XO, the Classmate PC, and models by Asus, Hewlett Packard, and Dell.

Our recent research in both Saugus and Littleton shows the benefits of netbooks, at least for students in the upper elementary grades. Each district is paying well under $300 per machine per student for the current version of Asus netbooks both are deploying; in Littleton, the amount is $275 per unit. For that, they get a laptop that weighs about 2.8 pounds, has a 10.1-inch screen, and has the capacity to carry out almost all the computer applications typically done in elementary school, with the exception of video editing (which could be carried out as needed on a few high-power desktops as an alternative.) The light weight and small size are advantages of the netbooks, as they put less burden on children who carry them around class and take up less space on students' desks. Students can easily make use of netbooks, books, and paper on a desk at the same time (see Figure 3.1), and teachers can easily peer over the tops of students' netbooks to maintain face-to-face contact. The low cost of netbooks made the Littleton and Saugus programs possible to launch at a time of tight budget restrictions in K–12 schools in the United States.

Our surveys, observations, and interviews indicated that teachers and students in both districts were largely satisfied with the performance of netbooks. The majority of teachers found their features, including screen size, keyboard size, and functionality, either as good as those of typical laptops or, if not as good, worth the cost savings they brought. In Littleton, for example, only about 15% of the teachers we surveyed believed that full-scale laptops would be preferable to netbooks in a one-to-one program.

This was in contrast, however, to attitudes toward the XO laptop that was used in Birmingham, where many teachers complained that its sluggish performance and lack of features hindered its use in the classrooms. This made clear to us that although there is a "good enough" revolution, there comes a point where cost savings and poor design lead to sharply

FIGURE 3.1. Student Using Netbook in Littleton

diminishing returns, which appears to be the case of the first-iteration XO laptop in U.S. schools (another XO model is now on the market and future models are being developed as well). The XO has not been adopted by any U.S. school districts other than Birmingham and, internationally, recently announced large programs in Argentina (3 million netbooks) and Brazil (1.5 million) have bypassed the XO in favor of the Classmate PC.

The growth of the netbook market has also put price pressure on traditional laptops. New models of laptops have emerged that have some of the features of typical laptops (such as optical drives), but at a smaller size and reduced cost. The lines between netbooks and laptops are thus merging, which means more options for one-to-one programs in schools.

FREE AND OPEN SOURCE SOFTWARE

The rise of netbooks has been accompanied by a growing use of free open source software. To understand this phenomenon, we start with some definitions. *Open source* refers to software in which the source code and certain rights normally reserved for copyright holders are provided under a software license that permits users to study, change, and improve the software (see discussion in Pfaffman, 2007). *Free software* adds two other conditions, depending on the sense of the term. In the generic sense ("free as in beer"), free software costs nothing to obtain or use. In the specialized sense ("free as in speech"), the source code of free software can be studied, changed, and improved, and the original or changed software can be freely redistributed for others to share. Practically, at least in terms of the education market, most open source software commonly used is also free in both senses of the word. The converse is not true, though, in that a number of companies distribute their software at no cost while maintaining proprietary control of the source code.

Open source advocates point to a number of its advantages compared to typical commercial software, especially when used with school netbooks, which would otherwise run on a version of Windows (Apple does not produce netbook computers). Open source Linux operating systems demand fewer computer resources than Windows, which means Linux-based netbooks run with more efficiency and stability than do Windows netbooks. In addition, Linux-based systems can be arranged to enable rapid recovery from system problems, thus eliminating much of the need to secure or manage the machines. Linux also provides for greater customization, allowing districts to develop a version of the operating system that best meets their needs, and has a simple interface for students and teachers. Finally, Linux is not prone to spyware, malware, or other malicious software that can attack Windows-based systems.

Saugus Union School District (SUSD) in California has been a leader in the use of open source software in education. SUSD implemented a netbook program for all its 4th-grade students in 2008–2009, based on a federal grant. The district's director of information services and technology, Jim Klein, purchases Asus netbooks for the program and has developed a customized installation of the Linux Ubuntu operating system for the netbooks, which he has made available to school districts across the country (for details, see Klein, 2010). The customized installation provides a total of 59 free software applications to support students' creativity and learning, all while keeping the installation as small as possible and reducing power usage. A customized interface was created with the goal of making the netbook as simple to use as a cell phone. In addition, the application files and user-created documents are saved on two different partitions of the computer storage so that in case the application software or operating system ever crashes, a teacher can reinstall the original software and settings while maintaining all of the user's files by simply holding down a function key and restarting the machine. Klein also customized the system for automatic online software installations, so that there is no need to manually install or update software on individual machines.

Klein spends a considerable amount of time each summer improving the operating system customization. This is a service not only to his own district, but also to a number of others across the country that make use of his Linux "build," including Littleton. However, beyond these summer updates, the system requires relatively little districtwide support, according to Klein. Though the netbook program brought in 1,500 new laptops, more than doubling the amount of district computers, Klein says that he hasn't had to add a single new staff person to keep the system up and running, as most problems can be resolved via simple reboots by teachers.

SOCIAL MEDIA

The World Wide Web was originally conceived with the goal of inspiring creativity and collaboration by the broad public. However, in the Web's first iteration, publishing online required specialized software and skills (see discussion in Warschauer & Grimes, 2007). Over the last decade, a new Web architecture has emerged, referred to as Web 2.0, that allows more interactive forms of publishing and participation through blogs, wikis, and social network sites. These participatory sites enable and rely on user-generated tagging of content, which itself can be aggregated into a user-generated taxonomy. The Web, which was thus once largely a read-only medium, has now become a read-write-link-share medium, where almost anybody can publish or network with others.

New social media are widely used by today's youth for hanging out with friends. However, these media can also enable learners to more easily create, publish, and link content and connect with mentors or experts. For example, most of the districts we have worked with recently are using blogging as a way to encourage student publishing of writing. A number of teachers are using Skype to make long-distance connections; for example, a teacher in Saugus told us how her class Skyped with a soldier stationed in Iraq as a way to get firsthand information about the U.S. presence there. Other classes are using online tools such as Prezi to create and share multimedia presentations.

Districts are setting up social media environments in a variety of ways. In Saugus, Klein has used the open source social networking engine ELGG to create two districtwide online learning communities, one for teachers and one for students. The online communities provide a platform that allows teachers and students share and contribute ideas, writings, files, podcasts, slide presentations, and other media as seamlessly as possible. Staff members use the site to share teaching ideas or resources, make administrative announcements, and collaborate on projects. Students can post writings, podcasts, and slide presentations on the districtwide blogs and also set up personal blogs related to their own interests. Students use avatars and first names for privacy, while teachers control which posts are accessible to the public and moderate comments. Parents, other relatives, and community members can respond and comment on posts that are publicly released. Some teachers set up voluntary reading blogs during summer to encourage students to read and discuss during the summer break, with many students participating.

Other districts use extant social media sites, such as Edublogger, on a districtwide basis, while others provide professional development to teachers about Web 2.0 in education and then encourage teachers to select whichever social media they wish to use in their classroom out of the wide range that are publicly available. But more important than the particular ways sites are accessed is the development of teachers' capacity to integrate social media in the classroom.

CLOUD COMPUTING

Moving content and communication to online realms allows schools to foster computer-mediated communication while easing up on the need to keep resource-hungry applications on individual computers. *Cloud computing*, which refers to the delivery of on-demand information technology services and software from distant online companies, provides an additional means to accomplish this.

One of the most common cloud computing resources in schools is Google Apps, which has been adopted statewide in Oregon and New York and is used elsewhere by individual districts and schools. Google Apps provides free access to all students in a K–12 district to Gmail (e-mail program), Google calendar (for keeping track of schedules and due dates), Google Talk (for making calls or sending instant messages), Google Docs (for word processing, spreadsheets, and slide presentations), Google Sites (for storing documents and Web content), and Google Video for Education (a video hosting and sharing service), as well as extensive online storage space. District adoption of Google Apps allows schools to provide communication channels such as e-mail in a secure way, since schools can set up filters for e-mail or provide teachers or district staff the ability to monitor activity. Google Apps also allows students to use productivity software—for word processing, spreadsheets, or slide presentations—in a flexible and collaborative fashion, as the Apps can be accessed from any computer with an Internet connection and since multiple users can collaborate on a single document either simultaneously or sequentially.

Littleton Public Schools has adopted Google Apps districtwide, and the services are being used extensively for collaborative writing and other activities. According to Dan Maas, chief information officer of the district, teachers and students find it much easier to share documents for collaborative writing, or for peer or teacher review, simply by clicking on Share in Google Docs than through other previous means. Some schools have decided not to replace their file servers since Google Apps fulfills the same need, thus, according to Maas, saving the district money. Amir Abo-Shaeer of the Dos Pueblos Engineering Academy, a program discussed in the next chapter, also reports that Google Apps plays a valuable role in his program. Students in the Academy carry out a great deal of collaborative writing to develop fundraising proposals, brochures, letters to businesses, work plans, and other documents, and also communicate closely via e-mail, with all this work being done with Google Apps.

MEDIA TABLETS

In spite of the many advantages of laptop and netbook computers for education, they also have a number of disadvantages. They can be relatively slow to boot up and launch programs. Their horizontal orientation and form factor restrict their usefulness as reading devices. Their size and weight can limit their portability inside or outside a classroom, and it is hard to use them when one is standing up (for example, to gather data or take notes while standing).

For these and other reasons, there has been a long-standing interest among educational technology specialists in the potential of mobile devices in class, which are smaller, lighter, more flexible, and potentially more interactive than laptops. Until recently, though, the enthusiasm of educational technology specialists has not been matched by ordinary teachers. For example, although several books promoted the role of the Palm handheld in schools (e.g., Curtis, Williams, Norris, O'Leary, & Soloway, 2003), the device was never widely adopted.

This situation has changed in recent years as mobile devices have become more sophisticated and user-friendly. iPod Touches, for example, have a great deal more capabilities than yesterday's Palm Pilots, including full wireless Internet access, a sophisticated touchscreen interface, and a host of downloadable educational apps, and they are being used with great enthusiasm in many classrooms across the United States. Most recently, the iPad, which combines the touchscreen interface, mobile operating system, and instant-on capability of an iPod Touch with a screen size comparable to netbooks, has caught the attention of many educators. Not to be confused with tablet PCs, which have existed for over a decade and are basically regular PCs with a stylus-type touchscreen, the iPad is the first of a new genre of *media tablets* with mobile operating systems (e.g., iOS or Android) and a multi-touch screen.

The iPad offers a number of advantages for education in comparison to netbooks or laptops, and some of these advantages are found in other media tablets, too. First, its lighter weight and orientational flexibility make it superior for digital reading or accessing of content. Second, its instant-on capability and fast switching among applications allows learning activities to proceed with less delay. Third, its touchscreen interface allows a high degree of user interactivity. Fourth, iPads are much more mobile than laptops, as students can carry them inside or outside a room without having to close and reopen the screen and can also use them for mobile data collection or notetaking. Finally, since it is inexpensive to develop applications ("apps") for iOS or Android, there is a rapidly growing amount of free or low-cost apps for media tablets, many of which are suitable for education.

iPads also have disadvantages compared to netbooks, at least in their first iterations. They are more expensive to purchase and more difficult to write and edit on, unless one gets an external keyboard at extra expense. Their lack of a computer-style file structure can make the organizing and sharing of student work more complicated, at least without establishing new file maintenance systems. And iPads are unable to access Websites that use the Adobe Flash multimedia platform, which is still common on many educational sites.

I have interviewed a number of K–12 teachers who are piloting iPads in instruction. Todd Ryckman of Dos Pueblos High, a school whose Engineering Academy is discussed in the next chapter, uses iPads with his students in a college preparation program and class called AVID. Ryckman believes that a major challenge facing high school students in the AVID program and his school overall is the development of academic literacy. As he explains, "students can read individual words on a page, but they don't really understand the importance of what they are reading." A major goal of his class is to help students become more analytic and reflective readers who can critically interact with the content of their texts. All his AVID students have iPads, which were purchased with funding from a local parcel tax to support secondary education. Ryckman carefully reviewed a considerable number of apps that he hoped could better promote academic literacy, and he found two that he says his students are now using very productively. iAnnotate is used at Stanford Medical Schools, which provides iPads to all its incoming students and is becoming popular in the medical community. It allows students to take text notes, highlight, underline, make free-form drawings, and insert bookmarks on PDF files; to more easily read PDF files through a variety of scrolling and zooming options; and to organize a PDF library by creating and managing folders, dragging and dropping files and folders, and searching one or all documents. Notes Plus allows students to take, edit, and organize notes that combine typed words, handwritten words, handwritten drawings, and audio recordings (of either lectures or student comments). Automated features of Notes Plus allow the recognition and conversion to digital format of shapes that are drawn (such as lines, circles, triangles, or squares) for better manipulation, as well as the auto-formatting of notes in a variety of specific formats. Ryckman's students are using these tools extensively, and also using the iPad for Internet searches, writing and printing papers (with the Pages app), and taking occasional end-of-class quizzes (with the eClicker app).

iPads are also being piloted at St. Margaret's Episcopal School in California in a program that we have been investigating through classroom observations and interviews. With a class set of laptops in every classroom, as well as a class set of iPads that are currently being used on a shared basis, the school provides an excellent laboratory for learning about the particular affordances of the iPad in comparison to laptops. Dylan Wade, a 6th-grade Earth Systems teacher, has been deploying the iPads extensively in his classes. Students use the iPads to read a free open source Earth Sciences textbook from CK–12 (see discussion below), investigate the elements and the composition of the Earth and galaxy via interactive apps, access the school's Angel e-learning platform, log and analyze lab data, and produce lab reports. Our observations suggest that the iPads are particularly helpful for laboratory work as the students carry the devices around to input data on the move. Students in the class were unanimous in telling us that they preferred using the iPads to the laptops due to their light weight, mobility, touchscreen, and apps; the laptops are thus rarely used when the iPads are available. School administrators do not believe that iPads can completely replace laptops yet, due to the superiority of the latter for writing, but the school may experiment with external keyboards to better test the potential of iPads for composing.

I also interviewed an algebra teacher in Long Beach who is piloting a new iPad version of a digital textbook, which I discuss in the following section.

In the long term, devices not yet invented may take educational technology in new directions. In the coming years, I expect there will be a lot of attention to the spaces where computers and mobile devices converge, certainly including media tablets and netbooks, including models with Google's new Chromebooks, and possibly other similarly sized devices, such as smartbooks (combining the operating system of a smartphone with the form factor of a netbook) or thin client laptops (which run little or any their own software but can operate server-based applications). Each of these devices has its own affordances that deserve exploration. In the end, though, it will not be any particular device that transforms education, but rather how teachers and learners make use of the devices.

DIGITAL CONTENT

In the 1980s and 1990s, writing for professional or academic purposes transitioned almost entirely from paper to screen—at least everywhere but in K–12 schools, which are still catching up. We now may be going through a similar transition from paper to screen for reading. Part of this involves the moving of traditional genres from print to device. For example, large numbers of people are choosing to buy and read books on Kindles or other eReaders rather than in paperback or hardback, and some digital textbooks are being developed that are essentially print textbooks in electronic format. But this transition also involves the development of new genres suitable for the screen, such as more interactive magazines or textbooks being developed for the iPad and other media tablets.

The development of digital educational content holds much promise for schools. Free or low-cost *online materials* can allow students access to individualized and differentiated instructional resources, often in multimodal or interactive format. *Open educational resources* can enable teachers, schools, and districts to access customizing high-quality learning material. And *digital textbooks* may be less expensive, more easily updated, and more interactive than printed textbooks, without weighing down the backpacks of students. We discuss each of these three types of digital content in turn.

Online Materials

All the one-to-one schools we have investigated make extensive use of online materials. These include general information Websites, the use of which is vital for student projects, as well as materials specifically designed for educational purposes. For example, teachers at individual schools such as North Park Elementary in Saugus (see http://tech4scholars.com/) and Hopkins Elementary in Littleton (http://5thfrogpond.wikispaces.com/) have created grade-level sites with links to free online materials in math, reading, and other subjects organized by course unit or content area. Students are then encouraged to explore these sites in their free time at the end of lessons. Students working in math, for example, will have listed a variety of sites, with animations, games, and activities, related to the particular content they are studying. These online materials often allow opportunities for learning experiences that simply can't be carried out with paper or books, such as watching or interacting with a simulation.

Among the most widely used educational resources in the schools we've observed are those produced by Discovery Education, including videos available through Discovery Streaming Plus and interactive instructional materials available through Discovery Science. The latter includes e-book reading passages, inquiry-based introductions, virtual labs to explore investigative design and scientific processes, inquiry-based exploration of science concepts, and interactive glossaries. Newport-Mesa Unified School District, which received an Enhancing Education Through Technology grant to establish a one-to-one netbook program in five schools that have large numbers of English learners, chose to use the Discovery Education Science materials, in part because they include audio, animations, video, and images, all of which are intended to make the material engaging and comprehensible to diverse learners. For example, Jenny Burks uses the program extensively with her 6th-grade class at Sonora Elementary, more than half of whom are English learners. In a recent unit, she first had students watch an interactive video on the layers of the Earth; while watching the video, they dragged words to parts of a model of the Earth and labeled its layers. They also watched a cave ecosystem video, which required them to look for and click on 20 specific items that appeared in the video. And while part of the class went on a field trip to a science camp, those who were unable to go instead worked on an activity in which they created their own ecosystem; students dragged different components, such as parks, ponds, or parking lots, into a wildlife area, and then checked repeatedly to see how changes in their design affected the survival of wildlife in the area. Through a pre- and post-test design funded by the National Science Foundation and in collaboration with the district, we are investigating how participation in such activities affects students' knowledge of science, academic achievement in science, writing ability in science, attitudes toward science, and technological proficiency compared to students in demographically similar schools that do not use the netbooks, and how these effects are mediated by students' English language ability.

Open Educational Resources

The resources discussed above are largely produced and controlled by commercial firms, even in cases where no-cost versions are available. In contrast, open educational resources (OER) are the educational equivalent of open source software. They are learning content or tools that are freely available to be used, remixed, improved, and redistributed. OER range from brief lesson plans created by teachers on particular topics to highly complex digital learning environments for teaching and learning science, math, social studies, or other subjects.

The National Science Foundation (NSF) has made the development of OER one of its priorities (NSF Task Force on Cyberlearning, 2008). Support from organizations such as the NSF and the Hewlett Foundation, as well as the contributions to OER projects from many scholars and education around the world, has allowed the development of a number of very high-quality OER. To get a sense of the type of OER being used in technology-rich schools, it is helpful to look at two examples, one in science education and one in computer programming.

Web-Based Inquiry Science Environment. The Web-Based Inquiry Science Environment (WISE) was developed to engage students in diagnosing problems, critiquing experiments, distinguishing alternatives, planning investigations, researching conjectures, searching for information, constructing models, debating with peers, and forming coherent arguments about science (Clark, Touchman, & Skjerping, 2009). The project began in 1996 at the Technology-Enhanced Learning in Science Center at the University of California, Berkeley, and has been further developed and designed by a large community of educational researchers. WISE is based on a series of online inquiry projects designed to meet statewide standards and complement the extant science curriculum. For example, in the "Sunlight, SunHEAT" project, students critique and compare energy-efficient homes from the Web, conduct an experiment that converts light energy to heat energy, and participate in online discussions about passive solar architecture (Slotta & Linn, 2009).

Students complete these projects by collaboratively considering and deploying online information, including the latest data from the Websites of governmental or nonprofit science agencies. To carry out a project, students click through an inquiry map, which is presented in the left-hand frame of the browser window and links to open materials, data visualization and modeling tools, or Web pages in the main part of the browser. Hints and notes are offered along the way to help students reflect on what they have learned, integrate ideas, and form predictions.

Projects in WISE emphasize visualization, simulation, and investigation with the goal of engaging students in scientific inquiry through challenging collaborative activities. A "Portal and Educator's Toolbox" provides teachers with a project library, a project editor (to customize existing projects or create new ones), and management tools to view and assess student work and provide feedback. All curricular units come with pre- and post-tests, which help guide classroom instruction and also provide data to the national WISE management team at the University of California, Berkeley.

Clark, Touchman, and Skjerping (2009) nicely summarize the affordances of software like WISE for teaching and learning. Such software serves to:

- *Script collaboration and activity structures,* by designing and orchestrating students' interaction with one another and the environment to best support learning;
- *Provide a knowledge base,* so that students have background information at hand to help them with complex activities;
- *Offer enriched representations,* using images, simulation, and video to help guide understanding;
- *Support data analysis,* through inclusion of tools, guidelines, and hints;
- *Foster collaboration,* with systems for both asynchronous and synchronous communication; and
- *Facilitate the co-creation and sharing of artifacts,* thus engaging students in proposing, supporting, evaluating, and refining their ideas.

Research suggests that these tools are effective. Students using WISE make gains from pre- to post-tests in their ability to reason about scientific topics and form coherent and connected explanations of their answers (Slotta & Linn, 2009), skills that are too frequently absent in science education in the United States.

The customizability of WISE and other OER makes them amenable to ongoing improvement. For example, building on the work done at UC Berkeley, educators at Vanderbilt University and Arizona State University created modules that included Spanish-language audio and texts to complement the existing English versions. An experimental study found that among Spanish-speaking students, those who had access to the bilingual version scored significantly higher on a delayed post-test than those provided only the English version, whether the post-test was given in Spanish or English (Clark, Touchman, & Skjerping, 2009). The study highlights one of the many advantages of digital materials in the classroom for English learners and at-risk students, especially those that can be flexibly used and adapted for the needs of diverse learners.

Scratch. While WISE represents an environment that is closely aligned with current standards in a particular subject, Scratch is a learning tool that can be flexibly used in many content areas, though it does not so closely match with any.

Developed by the Lifelong Kindergarten group at the MIT Media Lab, Scratch is a visual programming tool that uses text-based blocks that snap together to control on-screen objects called sprites. Unlike WISE, which is carried out through a browser, Scratch is a computer application that can be freely distributed and installed on any Windows, Mac OS X, or Linux computer. The program is aimed primarily toward children, and allows them to explore and experiment with the concepts of computer programming by using a relatively simple graphical interface. The programming language enables learners to create their interactive stories, animations, games, music, and art by importing and deploying graphical images, sound files, or items drawn by the user. It is designed to help users understand important computational and mathematical ideas, think creatively, reason systematically, and work collaboratively. A Website and online community provide users opportunities to view exemplars and tutorials, publish and share their creations, interact with others by posting comments on projects or messages on a community forum, and form small groups to either critique one another's projects or work collaboratively on new creations (Brennan, Monroy-Hernández, & Resnick, 2010).

Scratch has been used extensively in afterschool technology centers, most prominently in the scores of Computer Clubhouses funded by Intel (Kafai, Peppler, & Chapman, 2009). Research has documented the programming skills, media art awareness, new and traditional literacies, and self-confidence developed by youth using Scratch in those sites (Peppler & Kafai, 2007). For example, in one of our own recent studies, we reported on the experiences of Brandy (pseudonym), a young African American child with cognitive and learning disabilities who used Scratch extensively over a 2½-year period, starting at the age of 8 (Peppler & Warschauer, 2009). Brandy, who was tested as having an IQ of 60 and was unable to read or spell her name at the beginning of the study, leveraged the multimodal features of Scratch and the help of onsite mentors to teach herself programming. At the same time, her reading and writing ability accelerated as she encountered written words in scaffolded contexts (e.g., with images) and came to understand how symbolic pieces fit together to create meaning. The positive learning experiences and outcomes that we noted with Brandy have been observed in other afterschool contexts as well (see, e.g., Peppler & Kafai, 2007). Perhaps the one positive note from my visit to Birmingham was the enthusiasm and creativity of a teacher who set up an afterschool Scratch Club and of the students who participated in the club and presented their projects at an annual Scratch Day event.

The very flexibility of Scratch makes it somewhat more difficult to integrate into school curricula, which is largely based in the United States on established discrete subjects. Scratch can be used to support scientific or mathematical thinking, but the time and effort to teach the program and integrate it into instruction often make that challenging for subject-matter teachers, and neither does Scratch fit neatly into extant art or programming curricula. One place where we have noted some success with the use of Scratch in schools is in early elementary grades, where the curriculum is often more flexible. Scratch operates in Windows, Macintosh, and Linux environments, adding to its flexibility.

WISE and Scratch are just two of the hundreds of OER available to K–12 schools and teachers. Sites such as OER Commons, ReadWrite-Think, Curriki, and Connexions help teachers search for resources of interest to them by grade, subject area, and content.

Digital Textbooks

Textbooks remain the dominant way that learning materials are made available in U.S. schools, but printed textbooks have a number of drawbacks. They are expensive to print and distribute, and cannot be updated without publishing a new press run. Since printed textbooks are usually passed on from students one year to the next, students are typically forbidden to highlight passages or make annotations. Printed textbooks cannot be digitally searched, nor can they include animated, video, or audio content. And printed textbooks are heavy, making them difficult to cart back and forth from school to home or other locations for study.

Digital textbooks can potentially overcome many of these limitations. They are less expensive than printed texts and much easier to update. Annotations can be made without any physical degradation of a printed copy. A digital device weighing less than a single printed textbook, such as an iPad, can hold all of a student's books in electronic format. Digital texts can potentially include animations or video content, as well as mechanisms for students to communicate from within the text with mentors or peers. They can also include scaffolding for students with limited English language or literacy ability, such as rollover definitions or text-to-speech options. Digital textbooks also often come with accompanying online materials to assist instruction, such as individualized diagnosis and intervention systems.

Digital texts are far from perfect, of course. Most people find printed textbooks easier to browse, although that might change over time as

FIGURE 3.2. Example of Visual-Syntactic Text Formatting

Four score
    and seven years ago,
  our fathers
   brought forth
     upon this continent
   a new nation,
  conceived in liberty
   and dedicated
     to the proposition
    that all men
      are created equal.

hardware and software improve and users become more familiar with the experience of reading books digitally. They also require individual access to a digital device, which most U.S. schools do not yet provide for all students.

Digital textbooks are being used in several of the districts we have been researching. One of the netbook schools we observed in Littleton had recently replaced its social studies book with a digital text for cost savings. The book was available online and could be accessed either at school or at home (or, for those without home access, at the school library). On occasions when students without home Internet access couldn't use the school library, teachers would provide printouts of pages they needed. Teachers and students we interviewed commented positively on the book, and particularly on the text-to-speech option that was included. In Newport-Mesa district, students at Davis Magnet School use an online math text from Scott Foresman that is accompanied by instructional videos, online quizzes, and individualized homework assignments based on quiz results. A 5th-grade teacher there explained that these materials help ensure that each student does the follow-up practice best suited to him or her. A third school used an iPad version of a free online textbook from CK–12 (an organization discussed below).

The real power of digital textbooks will be seen when they are developed with the special interactive capacities of new media in mind. In this regard, two recent developments appear promising. First, a few companies are beginning to pilot the use of *visual-syntactic text formatting* (VSTF) in digital textbooks and online materials. Developed by a medical researcher, an ophthalmologist, and an expert in natural language software at a company called Live Ink, VSTF deploys a computer-based parsing engine to analyze each sentence in a passage and then reformat texts to "help the eye and the mind work together to build meaning as one reads"

(Walker & Vogel, 2005, p. 4; see example in Figure 3.2). With the syntactic complexity of sentences made more transparent by the cascaded indented formatting, fewer mental resources are needed to parse and understand sentences, and more mental resources can be devoted to text comprehension (Walker, 2007). Experimental and quasi-experimental research in both laboratory and classroom settings has demonstrated the superiority of text comprehension of material read in VSTF compared to traditional formatting, as well as higher reading comprehension scores on standardized tests for students who had deployed VSTF, with the greatest benefits accruing to English language learners (Walker, Schloss, Fletcher, Vogel, & Walker, 2005). Companies such as Holt, Harcourt, and Voyager Expanded Learning have partnered with Live Ink to incorporate the technology into some of their digital textbooks and online materials, and Live Ink also markets the software directly to school districts to use with other digital content.

Second, Houghton Mifflin is piloting a project that seeks to exploit the iPad's potential for digital reading and learning. The company's Holt McDougal Algebra 1 textbook incorporates immediate assessment results sent to teachers; instructional videos to teach or re-teach key concepts; vocabulary support throughout with links to a glossary with audio definitions; tips, hints, and links to assist students in acquiring help to understand lessons; step-by-step animations that demonstrate problem solving; scratchpad features that allow students to take written or audio notes within the application and bookmark sections for future reference; instantly graded quizzes at the beginning of chapters and strategic points throughout so students can review and practice particular areas of focus; a scientific calculator for completion of exercises and problem solving; and a graphic application to help students analyze and solve a range of functions, inequalities, and equations. The software is being piloted in the 2010–2011 school year in six middle schools throughout California. Classes were randomly selected at the schools to use the iPad curriculum, while other classes are using the text version of the same material. A team of researchers will study data collected from software logs to understand usage patterns and will combine measures of math achievement and program implementation to estimate the program's impact on learning, taking into account teacher and usage effects. Impact on learning may be minimal in the first year, as both teachers and students are just getting used to the tool, which was first handed out 2 weeks into the semester without any prior time for teachers to prepare, and as the first-generation features of the digital book are far from perfected. However, one of the pilot teachers, John Fox of Washington Middle School in Long Beach, told me that even the first iteration was helpful to his students, who are making good use of included instructional videos, graphing software, instant feedback from assessments, and solution sets to practice problems that include not only the final answers (as is typically found in print textbooks) but also worked-out examples of the problems.

California's Digital Textbook Initiative. Although commercial digital textbooks may prove to have advantages over printed versions, especially great hopes are held for the development of free digital textbooks designed and distributed as OER. In May 2009, Governor Arnold Schwarzenegger announced the state's Free Digital Textbook Initiative. The goal of the initiative was to provide school districts "high-quality, cost-effective options to consider when choosing textbooks for the classroom" and to support "a more interactive learning environment that leverages technology to meet the changing academic needs of California's students" (State of California, 2009). Since all textbooks used in California need to be reviewed by the state to ensure that they meet state content standards, the initiative established a review process for digital textbooks, to be managed by the California Learning Resource Network. So far, 33 completed digital textbooks have been recommended as meeting some or all state standards. Schools that adopt the digital textbooks must either ensure that students have digital devices at school and home, or provide printouts of the textbook material.

CK–12: Flexbook. A number of organizations have been working to develop free digital textbooks for California and other states, including two OER groups mentioned above: Curriki, a Silicon Valley–based nonprofit corporation, and Connexions, a nonprofit started at Rice University in Texas. Curriki and Connexions help produce and bring together a wide range of OER, including digital textbooks. In contrast, a third OER nonprofit called CK–12, also based in Silicon Valley, focuses more narrowly on the development and distribution of free digital textbooks, and has been especially productive in this regard.

CK–12 was founded as a nonprofit in 2006 with the specific mission of reducing the costs and improving the quality of textbooks in the United States and around the world. The organization focuses on science, technology, engineering, and mathematics, and has some 20 free secondary full-color textbooks available in these areas carefully aligned to state standards. The books are largely written by high school teachers and evaluated by reviewers and domain experts. About half of its books have already gone through the approval process for California, making the group the largest producer and distributor of approved digital textbooks in the state.

Any member of the public can register at CK–12's Website and then immediately have access to all of the organization's textbooks and chapters. Users can search for titles, subjects, and keywords or browse by subject area to find material, and then review either a summary or the content itself. They can read chapters through an online viewer, load them as clickable HTML files, download materials as PDF files, or drag and drop chapters from different books into their own unique book. Users can also revise chapters by deleting text, adding text, formatting text, or adding images or video. Any book accessed or created can be printed out or made available via e-mail to others, who themselves can read, print, or edit the material in all of the above ways. Most recently, ePub versions of the books suitable for the iPad and other eReaders can also be downloaded from the CK–12 site or from Apple's iBooks store.

A number of CK–12's books include optional video. Future plans include expanding the number of books, introducing simulations into some of them, adding features such as voiceover or other scaffolds for low-literacy students, and developing more interactive online content for STEM instruction.

Anyone who spends an hour or two exploring the CK–12 Website has to feel optimistic about the potential of digital learning. As the number of approved textbooks grows, the benefits of providing digital devices for all students will grow as well. Of course, as suggested by the rest of this book, education is about far more than providing the right learning materials, whether in print or online. We now turn to some outstanding examples of how digital devices and materials are put to use in instruction.

4

Exemplars

Example is the best precept.
—Aesop (6th-century B.C., reprinted in 1909)

In this chapter, we examine four outstanding K–12 programs. All four emphasize the use of digital media authentic learning, involving students in developing projects and products for distribution or use beyond the classroom walls. In two of the programs—both that started in upper elementary grades with one spreading to secondary school—this takes place largely through writing for public audiences. In the other two programs, in a middle school and a high school, it occurs through broader forms of experiential and constructivist learning. Each of the programs uses digital tools that are suitable for its goals: Netbooks in the two programs focused on writing, and laptops in the two other programs that require broader construction and design.

NETBOOKS AND WRITING

The first two programs I'll discuss have a great deal in common. Both deployed low-cost netbooks and open source software, focused on student writing as a lever for overall academic achievement, and both have achieved outstanding results in improved learning processes and outcomes.

Inspired Writing at East Elementary in Littleton

Littleton, Colorado, is a middle-income suburban community, largely White and English-speaking. Like many such suburban areas, it has pockets of economic, ethnic, and linguistic diversity. One such pocket in Littleton is found in the neighborhood of East Elementary School. In close proximity to low-income rental units, East has served many of the poor and immigrant families in the city. It was then designated as a school for English learners, thus bringing in more low-income non-English-speaking children from other areas of the city. In total, some 70% of East Elementary's students are English language learners and nearly all receive low- or reduced-price lunch.

The netbook program at East Elementary and other Littleton schools was designed in support of the district's Universal Literacy Framework, a curricular initiative developed under the leadership of Assistant Superintendent for Learning Services Connie Bouwman to guide "research-based, effective practice in reading and writing instruction" (Littleton Public Schools, 2008, p. 1). The literacy framework was based on a needs assessment of student performance performed by district leaders that, taking into account state and local assessments and teacher-assigned grades, developed detailed goals about how to improve student performance in the future (Littleton Public Schools, 2009).

A key component of the literacy framework was an emphasis on increased student writing, drawing on the work of Reeves (2002), who found that student writing, collaborative scoring of student work, and frequent formative assessment were all critical to academic achievement. A districtwide curricular approach to writing, based on Lucy Calkins's (1994) Writer's Workshop model, was implemented. Calkins's approach emphasizes authentic writing for a real purpose and audience. As she explains,

> For me, it is essential that children are deeply involved in writing, that they share their texts with others, and that they perceive themselves as authors. I believe these three are interconnected. A sense of authorship comes from the struggle to put something big and vital into print, and seeing one's own printed words reach the hearts and minds of others. (p. 3)

In alignment with this model, elementary school students in the district were to spend a total of 45–60 minutes a day on writing, broken up in three portions: (1) a 10- to 15-minute whole-class *Mini-Lesson* in which a teacher presents and students discuss models of writing, (2) a 30- to 35-minute *Writing Time* session in which students draft and edit their own written work while the teacher confers with individuals, and (3) a 5- to 10-minute time to *Share Writing* and receive feedback from others. Calkins's framework also includes specified components for reading instruction, including (1) a 15- to 20-minute *Shared Reading* period in which a teacher reads and thinks aloud to model what good readers do; (2) a 60- to 90-minute time for some combination of *Independent or Guided Reading*, in which students either read on their own or receive direct instruction in small groups in application of reading skills and strategies; and (3) a 15- to 30-minute *Word Work* session, in which students as individuals or in groups receive explicit instruction in phonics and vocabulary.

To support the literacy framework and Writer's Workshop curriculum, in an initiative called *Inspired Writing*, netbook computers were introduced in 5th grade in five low-performing district schools in 2008–2009. At four of the schools, this was done on a laptop cart model, with two or three teachers sharing a class set of netbooks. At East Elementary, since there were only two 5th-grade teachers and a second set of netbooks was available, each teacher was provided a full class set of netbooks for one-to-one classroom instruction throughout the day.

The Information and Technology Services Department in the district investigated different laptop and netbook models, and chose the lowest-costing one that they felt met instructional needs, an Asus Eee PC. An open source Linux operating system and other free open source software were chosen to provide a stable learning environment while minimizing costs. Since the netbooks were to be kept at school rather than taken home, the use of free cross-platform open source software and other free online resources helped ensure that students who had computers and Internet access at home could work on assignments there without having to purchase expensive software packages. Teachers in the program participated in a week-long training in the hardware and software, and, especially, how to integrate both into instruction. Following the training, teachers continued to collaborate across and within schools, with the two 5th-grade teachers at East, Chris Moore and Nicolette Vander Velde, co-teaching much of the time.

Students at East and other elementary schools use the netbooks throughout the school day, but especially in literacy instruction. For the Writer's Workshop, the netbooks provide an excellent tool for students to draft and edit their writing and share it with others. During *Writing Time* at East, the teachers select one student to write with the netbook connected to a projector, so the whole class can observe and later discuss a student's writing process. For *Share Writing*, students publish their work on a classroom wiki and blog. Moore and Vander Velde created a wide array of blogs that served different purposes. For example, one blog allows students to ask anonymous questions in relationship to a unit on human sexuality. Another blog was set up for a partner writing project with a school in Uruguay. Other blogs were established for literary analysis.

Moore and Vander Velde have continually sought other ways to help build connections through social media. For example, during *Shared Reading* time, the two teachers bring their classes together in one room and one teacher reads an interesting story out loud. Students then can comment either orally by raising their hands and being called upon, or by keyboarding their comments using a live blogging tool (CoverItLive) for an online discussion moderated by the other teacher. Moore and Vander Velde use this as an opportunity to get students to "push their thinking" about writing, by asking questions, both orally and via live blogging, about why the author of the story wrote something in a particular way. This use of computer-mediated conversation about readings serves two purposes in the classroom: It amplifies students' opportunities to participate in discussions while giving them additional chances to communicate their thoughts in writing.

Students at East and other schools in the district also have Skype discussions with experts around the world, including authors and photojournalists, and then blog about their discussions. We were told in interviews that having even one outside mentor involved in communicating with a class of students can have a big impact, as it helps students develop their writing with an audience and purpose in mind, and we noted students' great enthusiasm for writing in our observations and interviews.

The first year of the Littleton pilot program was highly successful, especially at East, the one school where the students had uninterrupted access to the netbooks. A total of 66% of the 5th-grade students at East scored advanced or proficient on the statewide writing test, compared to 58% of 5th-graders at the school the year before. A total of 72% of the 5th-graders there scored advanced or proficient in reading, compared to 52% of 5th-graders the year before. In writing and reading, a higher percentage of 5th-graders at East scored advanced or proficient than in the state overall, a notable accomplishment given that East is a designated school for English language learners.

In April 2009, the chief information officer in the district posted a query on the districtwide blog asking students' opinions about the laptop program and its relationship to writing. Students were involved in testing when the blog was first posted, and thus none responded for a few days, leading one adult to comment that he was cynical about the whole approach. Over the next few weeks, that brought forth a wave of student responses, with 168 comments left about the laptop program. Almost all were extremely positive, emphasizing themes such as the improved ability to draft and revise papers, opportunities to share and learn from others, increased access to information, more self-directed learning, greater engagement, and the perceived value of staying relevant in a technological world. Students were adamant that the program should continue.

Members of the Littleton Board of Education took note of the success of the program, as reflected both in student test outcomes and in the high quality of writing seen on the districtwide blog. Based on the success of the 2008–2009 pilot program, the program was extended in 2009–2010 into all 5th-grade elementary classes, 6th-grade reading classes, and 9th-grade language arts classes and, when positive results continued, the program was further extended in 2010–2011 to cover all grades from 5th to 10th. In the middle and high school levels, writing curricula were developed to go hand in hand with laptop use, similarly as had been the case for elementary schools. The district wants to extend use of the laptops to other middle and high school subjects once suitable curricula can be developed and funds can be raised for additional equipment.

Our observations, interviews, surveys, and test-score analysis in the district confirmed the positive results. Netbooks are used an average of nearly 2 hours a day in elementary school, and 1 hour a day in middle and high school (where they are so far confined to English class), with the principal uses being for writing and seeking information. The majority of teachers believe that their teaching is more effective with netbooks and they are able to use class time more efficiently. A majority of students report that they are more organized with netbooks, that schoolwork is more interesting, and that they write and revise more with netbooks. Interviews with students make clear that many, including immigrant students at East Elementary and other at-risk learners, are developing a strong identity as writers due to their use of the netbooks and social media for communicating with authentic audiences. Meanwhile, the test-score gains found in the pilot schools from 2008 to 2009 were also extended districtwide in 2009–2010. Using a quasi-experimental approach, we measured how much individual students' writing scores improved from 4th grade to 5th grade, and from 5th grade to 6th grade, in the first year of the netbook program (from 2009 to 2010) as compared to the changes in the same grade levels the year previously (from 2008 to 2009). Fifth-grade students improved upon their 4th-grade writing scores by an average of 28.12 points in the first year of the netbook program, as compared to by 22.54 points previously, a 25% increase in rate of growth. Sixth-grade students improved upon their 5th-grade writing scores by 11.48 points in the first year of the netbook program, as compared to 9.78 points previously, a 17% increase in rate of growth.

Not surprisingly, the district has begun to receive national attention and acclamation for the program's innovation and impact (e.g., Gabriel, 2010). But the most important acclamation came from the students themselves. A comment by Lupita (2009), a 5th-grader at East, epitomized students' excitement about the program:

I used to not like writing but now I keep looking at the time and inside I am saying, "Is it time for writing yet?" If you don't believe me come visit us. . . . You have to see it to believe it because your eyes will pop out.

SWATTEC at Saugus

The laptop program in Saugus Union School District on the outskirts of Los Angeles has much in common with that in Littleton. The district is in a middle-class suburban area similar to Littleton, but also with a considerable number of low-income English learners. As in Littleton, the program uses low-cost Eee netbooks and open source software; indeed, the customized version of Ubuntu used in Littleton was developed by Jim Klein, Director of Information Services & Technology in Saugus. And as in Littleton, the Saugus program focuses on writing as a lever to improve academic achievement. As Joan Lucid, District Superintendent in Saugus, explained to me,

I think writing is one of the higher thinking skills. If a child can write about what they learned, that means they had to synthesize it, summarize it, and have some kind of opinion about it. Whereas you can give a paper pencil exam with a bubble on it with pick a number or a letter, it's not about what they know; it's about what they don't know. We are finding that writing helps kids put their thoughts onto paper. I think it also gives us a lot of information about where some of those holes are.

The program in Saugus, called Student Writing Achievement Through Technology Enhanced Collaboration (SWATTEC), was funded by a federal Enhancing Education Through Technology grant. All 4th-grade students in the district have been provided a low-cost Asus Eee netbook since January 2009. Writing and other learning activities are supported by a wide range of open source software and a districtwide social media platform, described in the previous chapter. In the first 18 months of the program, a commercial online automated essay scoring/writing environment, My Access, was also provided for all students in the program. After the grant period ended, schools were left to their own resources to decide whether to continue using My Access; some did and some didn't.

Extensive professional development was carried out, including about 40 hours per year for all the teachers in the program over a 2-year period, and about twice that for one teacher at each school who served as a coach/mentor for others. Sessions addressed using netbooks, writing software, and social media in support of the *six traits writing approach* that focuses on students' ideas, organization, voice, word choice, sentence fluency, and conventions (Spandel, 2009).

The changes we noted in learning processes and outcomes in Saugus were similar to those in Littleton. Students used the netbooks about 2 hours per day. Main activities were writing, editing, and getting information from the Internet. Both students and teachers were especially enthusiastic about the benefits of new social media, especially through writing for blogs and wikis. As in Littleton, communication with faraway correspondents through tools such as Skype proved to be a powerful way to help connect students' learning to the world.

We carried out case study research in two schools, Skyblue Mesa and North Park Elementary School. Use of laptops in each illuminated how netbooks help meet the needs of diverse students. Skyblue Mesa is located in a low-income neighborhood. Approximately one-third of its students are Hispanic and half of those are English learners; the number of English learners in the school tripled from 2005 to 2009, creating challenges for teachers. Cheryl Cameron's 4th-grade class was typical of the diversity in the school. The class included four students in the district's Gifted and Talented Education (GATE) Program, eight students in special education, five designated as English language learners, and several students previously designated as English learners who still faced major challenges in their writing. Cameron found that the netbooks were of great value in differentiating instruction for her diverse students. For example, to provide enriched instruction to the GATE students, she would often assign them to work on advanced Internet-based research projects either after they had completed the regular class assignment or instead of it. English learners would also receive specialized scaffolding as appropriate, for example, through text-to-speech audio playback of difficult reading passages. And Ms. Cameron would use a variety of mechanisms, such as the My Access program or student blogs, to provide extensive individualized feedback on student writing. She would also use online programs such as SpellingCity to design individualized assessments for students.

North Park Elementary School had fewer English learners, but laptops helped to provide specialized scaffolding and instruction for them, through text-to-speech, bilingual dictionaries, and use of images. North Park also had a special education class whose teacher, Katie Buehler, was passionate about the value of the netbook program for her students. She explained that many students in her class had difficulty communicating with others, whether orally, due to autism or other disabilities, or in writing, due to fine-motor issues. She believed that the introduction of laptops made a huge difference for her class by creating a means and a focal point for student-to-student interaction, which was still carried out face-to-face, but around a computer. Ms. Buehler had long attempted programs in which "typical" students from other classes would come in and work in partnership with her students, but she found that this worked much more smoothly after the introduction of laptops, increasing the comfort of students on both sides of the equation. As she explained,

> Students this year are so willing to come from the general education classes. I think the computer is something they are confident and familiar with. They are very comfortable, and my [special education] students are very comfortable also. It gives them something to focus on outside of themselves and work together in harmony to accomplish a task. It takes them away from any social awkwardness that I have noticed before the computers. They would be very worried and afraid to come in before. They are very at ease. It's because the computers give them an equal playing field so they can come in and assist and help my students with little tasks and they feel so proud. My students are so happy to receive that assistance without feeling that they are somehow less. It's a huge equalizer. This is the second year, all new kids, and it's happened again. It really is an equalizer. I still find that to be amazing.

As in Littleton, information from surveys, observations, and interviews indicating improved learning processes was matched by excellent test score results. In fact, with the Saugus program in its second year in 2009–2010, the test-score improvements were even more impressive. We used a similar statistical approach in Saugus as in Littleton to measure the impact of the program on test scores. We compared changes in individualized students' English language arts test scores from 3rd grade to 4th grade in 2007 to 2008 (when 4th-grade students didn't have the netbooks), in 2008 to 2009 (when 4th-grade students had the netbooks about half the year), and in 2009 to 2010 (when 4th-grade students had the netbooks all year). Each successive year, the gains increased, with the gains on the reading portion, writing portion, and total English language arts test significantly higher after the laptop program was fully in place than before it started (see writing and English language arts score growth in Figure 4.1). The gains were sizeable, with students test scores increasing from 3rd to 4th grade at a 33% greater rate in English language arts after the program was implemented as compared to prior to implementation.

Further analysis showed that, when other factors were controlled for, students who used the netbooks the most in Saugus also had the highest

FIGURE 4.1. California Standards Test score growth (in points) from 3rd to 4th grade in Saugus before netbook program was implemented (2007–2008), during partial implementation (2008–2009), and following full implementation (2009–2010)

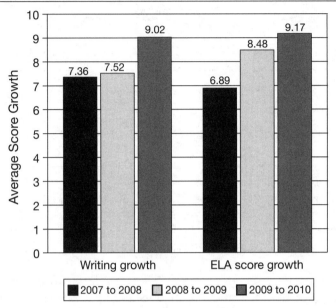

post-test scores. Finally, at-risk students—including low-income learners (i.e., those receiving free or reduced-price lunch), Hispanic students, and English language learners—all increased their improvement from 3rd to 4th grade after the netbook program was implemented at a faster pace than their counterparts (see Table 4.1). This is especially important because at-risk learners typically experience "a 4th-grade slump" in literacy as they transition from "learning to read" (decoding of simple texts with everyday vocabulary such as "dog," "cat," and "see") to "reading to learn" (comprehending texts with more complex vocabulary and grammar to understand new concepts in science, social studies, and other subjects; Chall & Jacobs, 2003). This 4th-grade slump is often a critical juncture on the way to eventual school failure and dropout. The fact that at-risk learners improved their growth in literacy at an especially high rate in the netbook program is thus a valuable outcome, and testament to the way that the Saugus program skillfully combined the appropriate hardware, software, curriculum, pedagogy, and professional development.

TABLE 4.1. English Language Arts Score Growth (in Test Score Points) from 3rd to 4th Grade Before and After Netbook Program in Saugus

	Free Lunch	*Non– Free Lunch*	*Hispanics*	*Whites*	*English Learners*	*Non– English Learners*	*All Students*
2007 to 2008	4.90	7.20	5.44	7.01	6.53	6.99	6.89
2009 to 2010	8.17	9.33	8.62	9.13	9.26	9.15	9.17
Change in Growth	+3.27	+2.33	+3.18	+2.12	+2.69	+2.16	+2.28
Percent Change in Growth	+66%	+13%	+58%	+13%	+42%	+31%	+33%

EXPERIENTIAL LEARNING

The two secondary school programs below are far apart in location and demographics, but are similar in the outstanding results and national acclaim they have received for innovative curricula based on experiential learning with technology. Experiential learning is similar to project-based learning, but the projects that students get involved in extend beyond the classroom. These experiential projects give students the opportunity to try out a variety of professional roles and create products of interest to communities outside the school.

Expeditionary Learning at King Middle

King Middle is a highly innovative Maine school that I extensively investigated earlier (then using the pseudonym of Castle Middle; see Warschauer, 2006). More recent interviews and test-score analysis indicate that the school is still an outstanding model for integration of new media in an experiential learning program.

King serves the most ethnically, linguistically, and economically diverse population of any school in Maine. Designated as a special school for English learners, about a quarter of its students are refugees and immigrants, principally from Somalia, Sudan, and other African countries, with smaller numbers from Latin American and Asia. The remaining students include youth from some of the most destitute housing projects of the Eastern seaboard, and middle- or upper-middle-class students from other surrounding neighborhoods.

In the school's earlier years, this socioeconomic stratification was reflected in seven distinct educational tracks, including one for the highly gifted, one for the accelerated (but not gifted), one for special education, one for non-English speakers, and several others calibrated by ability. A new principal was hired who had a mission of promoting an equal and quality education for all King students. The principal, Mike McCarthy, turned to a national pilot program developed by Outward Bound, and in 1992, King became one of nine "Expeditionary Learning Outward Bound" schools. The Expeditionary Learning program involved a complete remaking of the school and curriculum. Tracking ended and students from special education and English as a Second Language programs were integrated into regular classrooms to the maximum extent possible. All students were grouped into "houses" of about 60 learners and four main teachers, with the teachers in each house having broad autonomy over class scheduling. The houses developed highly flexible block scheduling, with classes meeting for different lengths of time on different days, with ample time built in for teacher collaboration. Most importantly, most of the academic work in the houses and school was integrated into 8- to 12-week interdisciplinary research projects. These projects, called learning expeditions, are designed to break with what McCarthy terms "the tyranny of coverage of curriculum," and instead involve students in collaborative inquiry on thematic issues, which, since 2002 (for 7th grade) and 2003 (for 8th grade), have been supported by students' individual access to Macintosh laptops.

Learning expeditions involve community projects that require students to do original research and create high-quality products for audiences beyond the classroom. The approach seeks to develop critical thinking and problem solving as elements of deep learning that prepares students for success in college and beyond. Emphasis is also based on creating a school culture based on strong adult-student relationships and positive character, with rigorous expectations for behavior and achievement. Students in learning expeditions have the opportunity to try on different professional roles and work closely with adult mentors.

Students in expeditions contribute to a comprehensive final product that requires each learner to create representations of the targeted knowledge and skills via both high-quality writing and craftsmanship. Student creation of art or multimedia thus always complements writing, rather than replacing it. All student writing done for the final product goes through an extensive review process, including self-editing, peer editing, teacher editing, and multiple revisions, giving low-performing students numerous opportunities to improve their work. The final product is multitiered, so that students who need extra support to produce their required portion can receive it while more advanced students can take on additional responsibilities related to research, editing, or multimedia production. Staff specialists in English language learning, special education, and basic literacy collaborate with the teachers to provide differentiated learning resources, experiences, and instruction that match the interests, abilities, and needs of all students, including multiple anchor texts, multiple students' roles in the expeditions, and varied learning activities, a level of individualization that is greatly aided by personal laptop access. Extensive and flexible use of digital media for research, writing, and multimedia production, especially individual student laptops and online resources, but also digital cameras, camcorders, and a small number of desktop computers equipped with specialized software, helps ensure that students develop technological skills to complement their academic ones. Finally, culminating events that include the exhibition of student work and a multimedia narrative of the expedition produced by students allow students important opportunities to showcase their work to family members and the community.

In one recent expedition, students interviewed Maine residents who were active in the civil rights movement, conducted research from primary documents of the era, and collectively wrote a 200-page book that they called *Small Acts of Courage*. A student-produced Website on the project includes a downloadable copy of the book, photos, a video of the culminating event, and an additional five-part video that documents the students' learning process. The latter video explains the detailed steps that students went through to convert interviews to stories, from review rubrics, to guided editing of other interviews, to collective analysis and scoring of model stories, to drafting, to peer and teacher editing, to final publication. In a second recent expedition, King partnered with university biologists to help students take soil samples from local farms and analyze the bacteria they contained. Working with community graphic artists, each student produced a pamphlet about particular bacteria that included both a written description and original artwork. In a third expedition called Creating Currents, students investigated ways to reduce their carbon footprint through energy audit data collection and subsequent analysis leading to informed conservation practices. They also investigated alternative energy production and public policy decisions involving alternative energy, and collaborated with experts in the areas of conservation, building products, design, and alternative energy to create a green building design. The expedition culminated with a competition of electricity-generating wind turbines built by the students.

Over the last few years, King has introduced more computer-related courses into the curriculum to supplement and support expeditionary learning. These include an introductory computer class and a digital music class in 6th grade, an informatics class and a scientific communication class in 7th grade, and a technology education class in 8th grade. Each of these courses allows more focused instruction in particular computer-related areas, and several also integrate project work. For example, in the technology education class, which focuses on building with wood, students go outside and collect wind data with their laptops, use that information to design small-scale model functional windmills, and then use specialized software to determine how much electricity would be generated by their windmills. The class ends with a contest in which the models are put outside to determine which generates the most electricity, with variables such as the number and angle of blades taken into account.

Students maintain digital portfolios of their work, which provide a means for ongoing assessment. King students also do very well on standardized measures of academic achievement. In spite of having many more African Americans, Hispanics, and limited English proficient students than the state average, King's students easily top the statewide average performance in both reading and math (see Table 4.2).

All Maine public schools have laptops for 7th- and 8th-graders, just like King. King's academic success with diverse students thus cannot be attributed to the hardware alone, which is shared by other schools. Rather, its success lies in how King has deployed the laptops in a highly innovative experiential learning program.

Engineering Academy at Dos Pueblos High

Dos Pueblos High School is located in the quiet suburban community of Goleta, just outside Santa Barbara, California. About one-third of its students are Hispanic and 11% are English learners. The school has a number of innovative programs and a well-deserved reputation for excellence. Not resting on its laurels, Dos Pueblos is constantly seeking ways to better prepare its students not only to enter college, but also to thrive in higher education and their careers.

The Dos Pueblos Engineering Academy was founded by Amir Abo-Shaeer, a physics teacher at the school who had previously worked as a mechanical engineer in the aerospace and telecommunications industries. As Abo-Shaeer explained to me in an interview, he felt his own education had taught him *about* engineering but had left him ill-prepared

TABLE 4.2. Academic Achievement Among 8th-Grade Students

	Percent Black or African-American	Percent Hispanic	Percent Limited English Proficient	Percent Economically Disadvantaged	Percent of Students Proficient in Math*	Percent of Students Proficient in Reading*
King Middle School	24	5	25	53	80	78
All Public Schools in Maine	3	1	2	40	69	59

*New England Common Assessment Program (State of Maine Department of Education, 2010)

to engage in the profession, and he sought to create a richer and more meaningful educational experience for his own students.

The Academy started in 2002 with two courses, one in engineering and one in computer science, and gradually expanded its courses and emphases. In 2005–2006, the program was fully implemented in its current form with the inclusion of a capstone Robotics course, in which seniors in the program participate as a team in the international *FIRST* Robotics competition. The competition requires them to design and construct a 150-pound robot to compete against robots from other teams in a game challenge that changes every year. For example, in the 2008–2009 school year, the competition involved the creation of a robot that could move in a multidirectional fashion and then shoot balls over a wall into a basket. Some 2,000 teams from around the world compete in *FIRST* Robotics, starting with a 6-week build season and followed by a series of regional and international matches.

Most robotics teams are formed on an extracurricular afterschool basis. The Dos Pueblos Engineering Academy has integrated the robotics competition into the school curriculum. As at King Elementary, the Engineering Academy gives students chances to try out real-world professional experiences, but in a more in-depth way. First, from 9th to 11th grade, students take a variety of traditional and innovative courses, with project work most extensively integrated into a special 3-year course that is discussed in the section on curriculum in the next chapter. Then, building on the mechanical, electrical, programming, and design skills that the students develop in the first 3 years of the program, the final 12th-grade build season is intended to provide students with an experience that simulates what it is like to work for an innovative engineering company. Students must lead an extensive engineering project that depends on a high degree of teamwork, strategy, construction ability, and understanding of engineering and science concepts, including elements such as managing budgets, working toward deadlines, making formal presentations, building Websites, and taking a project from concept to completion. Mentors are encouraged to participate, and the Engineering Academy has recruited several from the community to assist, thus furthering the opportunity of students to learn from close collaboration with experts.

To say that the Engineering Academy has been a success would be an understatement. The school's robotics team has twice won the Motorola Quality Award for the best-designed robot in the competition and most recently advanced to the quarterfinals in the national championship. There is fierce competition to enter the Engineering Academy from students throughout the school district as well as from local private schools. The Academy has been especially successfully in changing girls' attitudes toward engineering; in the first year of the program, only two girls sought to participate, but in the most recent senior class females made up a majority of the 32 students. Abo-Shaeer and the Academy have now received a $3 million grant from the state to build a large new facility that will make possible a dramatic expansion of the program, so it can reach the larger number of diverse students who have been attracted to it; matching funds of $3 million for a total of $6 million were raised locally. Graduates of the program are in high demand both for university engineering programs and for internships with firms (Bascomb, 2011). Finally, Abo-Shaeer was named as one of 23 national MacArthur Fellows for 2010, an unrestricted award of $500,000 given for extraordinary originality and dedication in creative pursuits. Abo-Shaeer has set the goal of extending this kind of rigorous project-based learning to other schools in California and across the nation and, toward that end, is planning to invite teachers from other districts to observe or intern at the Engineering Academy, and also send Academy students to local elementary schools and junior high schools to get them interested in engineering, technology, and science.

This is being accomplished at a school that, like others in cash-strapped California, has had difficulty increasing the number of computers or updating its outdated computer labs. To overcome this, students in the Academy bring their own laptops to school for advanced course work and the robotics activities, with the Academy seeking a way to provide a laptop to families that cannot do so. This is facilitated by a district policy that allows students to bring any digital device to schools and connect to the district network, as long as the device is used for learning purposes. Students in the Academy also make extensive use of free online or cloud-based programs, such as Google Docs, for collaboration.

The robotics project at Dos Pueblos, and the entire Dos Pueblos Engineering Academy, matches well with the philosophy of *FIRST*, which was summarized by Woodie Flowers, professor emeritus at MIT and *FIRST* Robotics co-founder:

> Training and education are very different. Training is a commodity. Education is the part that confers comparative advantage. Much of what we call engineering education is in fact training and poorly done. Learning calculus is training. Learning to think using calculus is education; learning spelling and grammar is training. Learning to communicate is education; learning a CAD (computer-aided design) program is training. Learning to design is a much more complex, sophisticated thing; learning the parts is training. Learning the synthesis and whole is education. It's not clean. The boundary is clearly fuzzy. Once you could be trained to be a professional if you know things, that was enough, but information is ubiquitous, you can't have an advantage in society because you know something. (quoted in Bascomb, 2011)

The kind of high-quality experiential project work carried out at King Middle and Dos Pueblos High is sometimes found in elite private schools or very well-funded charter schools, such as the High Tech High charter school in San Diego that has received funding from the Gates Foundation. Yet King and Dos Pueblos are ordinary public schools that have achieved their success due to the inspiration and perspiration of their administrators, teachers, parents, and students. Their examples can be replicated elsewhere, especially if we better understand the processes involved in innovative educational design.

5

Designs

Education is not the filling of a pail but the lighting of a fire.
—William Butler Yeats (quoted in Fitzhenry, 1993, p. 138)

The examples from the previous chapter make clear how computers themselves are only a small part of educational reform with technology. In each of those four schools, computer use helped improve learning because of the way it contributed to a well-designed educational program, with innovative curriculum, pedagogy, and assessment. In this chapter, I discuss these elements of educational design, both separately and in combination, and then critique an alternate design for learning with digital media.

CURRICULUM

K–12 curriculum in the United States has not changed much from the industrial era of a few decades ago and still reflects that era's mindset. It emphasizes accumulation of a large number of discrete facts and skills that will somehow be later assembled together. Indeed, even the highest-level courses in U.S. schools—the Advanced Placement (AP) courses that provide college credit to high school students—are typically a "mile wide and an inch deep" (Landsberg & Rathi, 2005, p. B1), a problem that has gotten the attention of the College Board that administers the AP tests (Drew, 2011). K–12 teachers are thus constantly working to cover the curriculum, rather than to help students develop the kinds of deep understanding and expert thinking needed in a post-industrial knowledge economy.

Of the efforts to reform schools with technology that we have researched, the most successful ones have put a good deal of effort into curriculum development. In Littleton, the laptop program worked well because it matched with and contributed to the district's universal literacy program and its Writer's Workshop component. Aspects of the curriculum were adjusted and improved for a one-to-one program. So, for example, whereas the Writer's Workshop's *Share Writing* time is usually accomplished by posting work on bulletin boards, reading it aloud, or passing it around, teachers in Littleton implement shared writing through the use of blogs and wikis.

In King Middle School, the Expeditionary Learning model provides a radically different approach to curriculum, with the content of each of the main subject areas taught in an interdisciplinary fashion through learning expeditions. Curriculum development at King is an ongoing process (for a detailed description, see King Middle School Expeditionary Learning Planning Group, 2009) carried out by the four main content teachers (in math, language arts, social studies, and science) in each house of 60 students with the support of specialists in English language development and literacy. The first step involves developing a compelling topic that targets the content and skills that students need to know at their grade level, is engaging to students, addresses community issues, provides opportunities for in-depth investigations, and provides opportunities for students to identify with or consider multiple perspectives. Guiding questions are developed that synthesize the big ideas and both require and scaffold students to engage in complex thinking. Additional steps include designing the comprehensive final product, choosing the professional roles that students will assume, identifying and organizing major learning resources, developing a shared team calendar, and planning a culminating event. Each house also develops its own flexible-schedule calendar for the school year, which both ensures that blocks can be divided up in a way to best support successful completion of the expeditions and allows teachers to include more collective planning time than is typical in many states.

Curricular reform is often most challenging at the high school level, due to the atomized nature of students' class schedules and the need for students to master a great deal of specified academic content in each of their many courses. For that reason, the curriculum development that has occurred at the Dos Pueblos Engineering Academy is especially interesting. A look at what the problems in the school curriculum were and how they have been addressed gives an idea of what kind of restructuring is necessary to transform schooling, especially at the high school level, and what kind of challenges make that restructuring difficult. As Academy director Abo-Shaeer explained to me, the curriculum has been difficult to change, both due to California's standardized testing regime, which motivates coverage of a wide area of content in a short amount of time, and also the curriculum guidelines from the University of California that

FIGURE 5.1. Prior Curriculum for Dos Pueblos Engineering Academy (Project-Based Courses in Italics)

9th Grade	10th Grade	11th Grade	12th Grade
English 9	English 10	English 11	English 12 or AP
Geometry	Algebra/Trigonometry	Pre-Calculus	Calculus
Engineering Physics	*Engineering/ Computer Science*	AP Physics	*Advanced Engineering Physics*
Foreign Language	Foreign Language	Foreign Language	AP Computer Science, AP Chemistry, or elective
Visual/ Performing Arts	World History AP	U.S. History AP	Gov AP/Econ
P.E.	P.E.	Elective/ Health	Elective
	Biology		*Robotics*

determine which high school courses match UC admission requirements. These UC guidelines were set up with the best of intentions—to help ensure that all UC applicants are well prepared for rigorous college study—but they made difficult the kinds of reform that Abo-Shaeer sought.

The Engineering Academy grew on top of an extant academic program, with new courses in engineering and robotics inserted into students' crowded academic schedule. Abo-Shaeer explained to me that he wanted to integrate more project work in conjunction with a rigorous curriculum. Abo-Shaeer first worked to create a theoretical, but hands-on, Advanced Engineering Physics class taught in 12th grade (see Figure 5.1) that served as an accompanying course to the 12th-grade elective course in Robotics. It took Abo-Shaeer more than 2 years to get the University of California to approve it as meeting subject-area requirements in laboratory sciences, since it deviated from the way physics courses are ordinarily taught in high school, but eventually approval was given.

A more challenging problem was found in students' first 3 years (grades 9 to 11), before they joined the 12th-grade robotics team. As seen in Figure 5.1, students were only able to take one project-oriented course during the entire 3 years due to the need to complete more traditional course requirements. The schedule caused several problems, according to Abo-Shaeer. First, since students had to take the state's standardized exam in physics at the end of the 9th-grade Engineering Physics class, it was necessary to squeeze an entire year's worth of facts and content into that 1 year, which allowed little time for project work. (Since the "year-end" testing is actually done in April, rather than June, this problem was further exacerbated.) This resulted in all project work being done in the second year. But, with all project work squeezed into that year, there was little time for necessary direct instruction in the Year 2 Engineering/Computer Science Course. In other words, instruction and project work were artificially separated from each other, with one carried out in Year 1 and the other carried out in Year 2. A second problem was that, since some similar principles and tools were taught in different classes that were not always taken by the same students in the same sequence, there was wasted time due to repetition. For example, basic soldering had to be introduced in both the engineering course and a visual arts course. A third problem was that principles of art and design were marginalized in the curriculum, since students did not have time to take art classes every year, yet design principles and processes are critical to innovation in today's world.

Abo-Shaeer sought ways to better integrate instruction in engineering, physics, and art across the course schedule so as to overcome these problems. A not uncommon approach to promoting interdisciplinary work is to have concurrent team teaching within two or more courses of one academic year. This is essentially what is done at King Middle School, where teachers across several subject areas coordinate their work on learning expeditions. Abo-Shaeer considered the possibility of following this model by having students take an engineering, physics, and art class simultaneously in 1 year. In that case, though, even if students found room for all these courses in 1 year, it wouldn't solve the problem of a single year not being sufficient to cover both content and project work. And, due to other requirements, students at California high schools intending to go to university do not have the space in their schedule to take separate courses in engineering, physics, and art year after year.

Abo-Shaeer worked with the University of California and finally got its approval for a very rigorous but creative curriculum reform that addresses all these problems. In the new schedule, physics, engineering, and art will be taught together in an interdisciplinary manner, but rather than doing that for three periods in one year, it will be done during one period for 3 consecutive years, from 9th to 11th grade (see Figure 5.2). All students in the Academy will now take this 3-year integrated physics/engineering/arts course that offers fractional credit in each course each year, with a full year's worth of credit being accumulated in each of the three subject areas by the end of 3 years. In that way, it will be possible to cover each of the subject areas (physics, engineering, and arts) in a non-repetitive, integrated, and recursive fashion *and* include substantive proj-

FIGURE 5.2. New Curriculum for Dos Pueblos Engineering Academy (Project-Based Courses in Italics)

9th Grade	10th Grade	11th Grade	12th Grade
English 9	English 10	English 11	English 12 or AP
Geometry	Algebra/Trigonometry	Pre-Calculus	Calculus
Physics/Engineering/Art 3-year sequence			*Advanced Engineering Physics*
Foreign Language	Foreign Language	Foreign Language	AP Computer Science, AP Chemistry, or elective
Biology	World History AP	U.S. History AP	Gov AP/Econ
P.E.	P.E.	Elective/Health	Elective
			Robotics

ect work during each year of the program. What's more, the 100 students in the program will all take the course during the same period, with the three teachers (in physics, engineering, and arts) teaching the group, with the assistance of mentors from outside the school as well as from students from previous years in the course (e.g., 10th-grade students serving as assistants for the 9th-grade course, and getting elective credit for that). Students will take the state physics test at the end of the third year, rather than the first year, by which time they will be fully prepared without having to sacrifice the need for project work. Since all of this will take place during one class period, they will be able to take other science classes (e.g., life sciences, biology) in 9th and/or 10th grade, and take the state science exam in those subjects during those years.

The 3-year curriculum that has been developed and now approved is both rigorous and comprehensive, and includes the purposes, outlines, key assignments, laboratory activities, and assessments for each year, with the latter including the development of digital portfolios and the carrying out of in-depth real-world projects. Early projects might be the development of toys or games that would be donated to needy children. Later projects, developed over 2 to 3 years, might include the collaborative design, creation, and installation for a local organization of a kinetic sculpture that includes a touchscreen video with illustration of the science behind its components.

Although *FIRST* Robotics has high school teams throughout the United States (and, indeed, world), they are almost exclusively extracurricular. According to Abo-Shaeer, this lack of institutionalization results in many teams disbanding after a couple of years, as they rely entirely on volunteer labor. Integration of the Robotics course into the curriculum—and, indeed, helping build an entirely new curriculum around it—has taken a great deal of effort and expertise at Dos Pueblos, but such an effort is essential to the kind of long-lasting educational transformation that Abo-Shaeer is promoting and that our schools badly need.

Abo-Shaeer hopes to extend this interdisciplinary experiential approach to other subjects—for example, by developing sequences that combine English, economics, and business. The full description of the 3-year engineering/physics/art curriculum, which Abo-Shaeer shared with me, makes evident the tremendous amount of talent, thought, and work that went into it. One of the great shames of No Child Left Behind is its impact in deprofessionalizing teachers, by directing almost all their attention to achieving very narrow goals based on outdated curriculum and stilted pedagogy. The efforts put in by Abo-Shaeer and his colleagues at the Engineering Academy are indicative of the higher-level professional involvement needed of teachers if we are to develop the curricula, pedagogy, and assessment required for 21st-century learning.

PEDAGOGY

Just as curriculum needs updating for a post-industrial information society, so does pedagogy. In some ways, the kinds of teaching that are needed are not that different from what Dewey was promoting when he wrote *Democracy and Education* nearly 100 years ago, when he was presumably promoting a new form of "20th-century learning." In between, though, we got derailed by an industrial model of teaching that was in line with the industrial model of curriculum discussed above. The failures of that model in relationship to new technology use are illustrated by the anecdote of the veteran teacher who allegedly boasted:

> Don't tell me about educational technology. I've been using it for decades. In fact, I have all my lecture notes written down on a huge rolled transparency. Every year, I stand in front of the class and just roll the transparency, and the students copy down the information in their notes. And that's how I can tell how well the class is going. The faster I can roll, the better it's going. (quoted in Warschauer, 2003, p. 119)

If we are to give up this model of pedagogy—in which material passes from the notes of the teacher to the notes of the student without entering the minds of either—what, then, shall replace it? The common educational technology mantra is that a teacher in the 21st century should become a *guide on the side*, rather than a *sage on the stage*. There is certainly good reasoning behind this; the kinds of exciting project work highlighted in the last chapter could not take place if students were simply listening to lectures all day. However, like many other mantras associated with technology, this one is subject to misinterpretation, as can be seen by an earlier study of what is called *network science*.

Launched in the United States in the 1980s, network science projects involved teams of children in classrooms throughout the United States and the world. The idea behind the program was that children would learn through collecting scientific data and sharing it on the Internet, providing a wealth of scientific information to promote constructivist learning. Typical network science projects involved measuring the acidity of local rainfall, tracking migrations of birds, or recording local weather conditions. In these projects, online information developed by the national or international project organizers provided instructions and supplemental materials. Chat rooms, bulletin boards, discussion forums, and e-mail lists provided opportunities for long-distance interaction.

Although these projects were presumed to support constructivist learning in the classroom, no one had really measured their impact until the late 1990s, when a research organization, known as TERC, carried out a 5-year study of network science programs. TERC had been instrumental in launching and leading several network science programs, including some of the ones under investigation, so presumably the TERC researchers were hoping to find positive results. However, their final report (Feldman, Konold, & Coulter, 2000) offered a devastating critique of the typical practices of network science. They found three main trends. First, students tended to upload data to the Internet without even bothering to download others' data. Second, when they did download data, they often had no idea how to analyze or interpret them in any meaningful way. And third, although students reported that they enjoyed communicating with other students online, it was found that this interaction was usually about personal and social issues that had very little to do with science.

Some network science projects were successful, but only in cases where strong instruction was already taking place *inside* the classroom. The readings and guidelines provided online were in and of themselves shown by the study to be ineffective in teaching children how to do science. Classrooms that depended principally on these online resources benefited little. But in classrooms where there was a very strong in-class teacher-led component, with students taught how to collect, analyze, interpret, and discuss data before they ever went online, the Internet-based communication and resources added additional value. In other words, the central feature enabling effective use of Internet-based materials and distance communication was a strong local teacher.

The lessons of network science have appeared again and again in our own research. Computers and the Internet help amplify good teaching. A good illustration of the kind of instructional leadership required for teaching with technology was seen at East Elementary in Littleton, a school we have previously discussed. As noted earlier, each writing lesson was divided into three parts: a *Mini-Lesson, Writing Time,* and *Sharing Time*. During the mini-lesson, in line with Writer's Workshop principles, all the students sat on the floor as the teacher discussed a particular genre of writing and how it is constructed. As seen in the example in Figure 5.3, Ms. Vander Velde is not acting during this period as a guide on the side. The mini-lesson is brief, but it is critical to the entire writing session, as it helps provide learners with an understanding of how to construct particular genres. Then, during the writing time, the teachers worked carefully with individual students at a projector, so that other students could witness the advice they were giving. The teachers served as very thoughtful and critical readers, continually urging students to push their thinking in their writing and offering suggestions on how to do so. As for the shared writing time, students posted on numerous blogs that the teachers had designed to facilitate more interaction among peers and with outside mentors. The teachers at East thus wore many hats—as lecturers, mentors, orchestrators, designers, and, yes, sometimes as guides on the side.

We found the same things in all the good schools we have observed over the last decade—good learning with technology stems from good teaching. And good teaching sometimes involves being a guide, but often involves much more that that.

Technological Pedagogical Content Knowledge

What kind of knowledge and skills does it take to be a good teacher with technology? Mishra and Koehler's (2006) model of *technological pedagogical content knowledge* (TPACK) helps answer this question. The roots of the TPACK model lie in an old debate over whether good teachers principally need *content knowledge* (such as an understanding of mathematics or science) or *pedagogical knowledge* (i.e., a generic understanding of issues of student learning, classroom management, lesson plan development and implementation, and student evaluation). Shulman (1986) addressed this dichotomy by introducing the notion of "pedagogical content knowledge," which he defined as "the particular form of content knowledge that embodies the aspects of content most germane to its teachability" (p. 9). Pedagogical content knowledge includes two distinct but overlap-

FIGURE 5.3. Ms. Vander Velde Teaching Writing at East Elementary

ping components. On the one hand, it refers to an understanding of the most useful forms of representation of the ideas in a particular subject or discipline, that is, the most powerful analogies, illustrations, examples, explanations, and demonstrations to make the subject comprehensible to others. Shulman argued that since there is no single most powerful form of representation, an expert teacher needs to have at hand a wide array of alternative forms, some of which derive from research and others from the wisdom of practice. The second component of pedagogical content knowledge is an understanding of the conceptions, preconceptions, and misconceptions that students of different ages and background most frequently bring to the learning of topics within a subject, and strategies to reorganize the thinking of learners with these misconceptions.

Pedagogical content knowledge thus represents an intersection of content knowledge and pedagogical knowledge. The implication is that teaching that is based on generic pedagogical knowledge (but not on content knowledge) or on content knowledge (but without any pedagogical knowledge) will be inferior to teaching based on pedagogical content knowledge.

Mishra and Koehler extended Shulman's model to develop the TPACK concept. As they explain, technology is typically viewed as "a separate set of knowledge and skills that has to be learned," and that the relationship between those skills and "the tried and true basis of teaching (content and pedagogy)" is either unrecognized or "considered to be relatively trivial to acquire and implement" (pp. 1024–1025). As a consequence of this perspective, teacher training programs and workshops are often designed to focus on the learning of specific hardware and software skills, with insufficient attention to their relationship to content and pedagogy.

The TPACK model (see Figure 5.4) brings technology into the fold. Technology is viewed in this model as intersecting with both content knowledge and pedagogical knowledge. At one intersection, technological content knowledge involves an understanding of how subject matter is changed by the application of technology. A chemistry teacher, for example, should know how new types of hardware and software are used in chemical analyses, while an English teacher should be familiar with new kinds of online writing genres. At the other intersection, technological pedagogical knowledge includes generic knowledge of how technology can transform pedagogy through the use of tools such as discussion forums.

TPACK represents the intersection of all three forms of knowledge: technological, pedagogical, and content. It is, according to Mishra and Koehler,

> the basis of good teaching with technology and requires an understanding of the representation of concepts using technologies; pedagogical techniques that use technologies in constructive ways to teach content; knowledge of what makes concepts difficult or easy to learn and how technology can help redress some of the problems that students face; knowledge of students' prior knowledge and theories of epistemology; and knowledge of how technologies can be used to build on existing knowledge and to develop new epistemologies or strengthen old ones. (p. 1029)

Returning, once again, to our example from East Elementary, TPACK can be represented by knowledge of the particular ways that the use of blogs can help foster students' sense of audience and purpose in writing. In other contexts, it might refer to knowledge of the way that sketching software can help challenge students' misconceptions about geometry, or of how watching and responding to online simulations can build learners' understanding of key physics principles.

FIGURE 5.4. Technological Pedagogical Content Knowledge (TPACK)

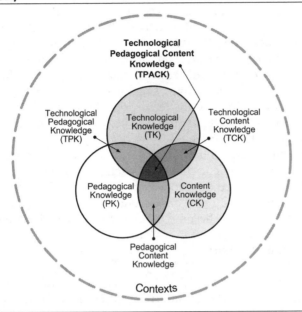

Source: Koehler & Mishra (2010)

There are, of course, many terrific teachers who implement the principles of TPACK without necessarily being familiar with its name. In that sense, the TPACK model is simply a way of making explicit what many outstanding teachers are doing implicitly. It is a helpful model, though, because it calls attention to the ways that technology is too frequently separated from content and pedagogy and makes explicit the need for the integration of all three in instruction. Littleton and other school districts have started to successfully use the TPACK model as a framework for teacher training, as will be seen in the following chapter.

ASSESSMENT

Educational assessment is a multibillion-dollar industry in the United States. Unique among developed countries, the United States puts students through an extensive series of high-stakes standardized tests every year, the results of which can be used to punish schools and their staff. Our decade-long obsession with testing has done little to increase educational performance or narrow gaps by demographic group in the subjects that are tested; we are making progress in increasing performance and narrowing gaps in these subjects, but no faster than we were before No Child Left Behind began (Ravitch, 2010). However, this testing focus is almost certainly having negative affects in areas not regularly tested, such as the teaching of the arts, since these are increasingly ignored. The narrow emphasis on standardized tests is also a major impediment to reforming schools with technology, since teachers widely report that the pressure of standardized exams leaves them little time or flexibility to introduce more innovative instructional activities with digital media (see, e.g., Warschauer et al., 2004).

Assessment policies and practices in the United States are thus badly in need of reform. Indeed, changing assessment policy is arguably the linchpin in improving U.S. schools, since assessment drives everything else that happens in K–12 education. Assessment needs to be changed in two critical ways: It must become more *performative* and more *formative*.

Performance Assessment

To get a driver's license in the United States, you must pass two tests: a written multiple-choice test on driving rules and an actual driving test on the road. The first measures what cognitive scientists call declarative knowledge. The second measures something much more important—how you can take knowledge and skills and apply them in a meaningful real-world performance.

The tests that dominate our educational system have much more in common with the written multiple-choice road rules test than with the performance-based driving test. This is certainly true of the high-stakes standardized tests that are so influential in today's educational climate. And because schools are so focused on preparing students to take high-stakes tests, similarly narrow approaches to testing dominate classroom assessment as well. There is growing recognition of the limitations of the kinds of tests we most frequently use, but we continue them anyway, in part because they are easier and less expensive to administer and score than more authentic assessments. In that sense, we are like the proverbial drunk who looks under the streetlight for his lost keys, even though he misplaced them elsewhere, "because the light is better over there," as the joke goes. In this case, though, the joke is on us, because we similarly persist in searching/assessing where it is easier, even if the chances of finding what is really meaningful there are low.

What, then, would "driving test" types of assessment look like in education? That would differ somewhat from classroom contexts to standardized assessments. As to the former, Wiggins and McTighe (2007) call for what they name *cornerstone assessment* tasks, that is, worthy authentic performances that are reflective of the key challenges in the subject. They provide examples of such challenges in a number of disciplines:

- In science, the design and debugging of significant experiments
- In history, the construction of a valid and insightful narrative of evidence and argument
- In mathematics, the quantifying and solving of perplexing or messy real-world problems
- In world language, the successful translation of complex idiomatic expressions
- In communication, successful writing for specific and demanding audiences and purposes
- In the arts, the composing/performing/critiquing of a sophisticated piece (pp. 42–43)

McTighe and Seif (2010) help deconstruct what the distinguishing qualities are of these kinds of cornerstone tasks. First, they reflect genuine real-world accomplishments and are set in authentic contexts. Unlike items typically found on standardized tests, they are contextualized in a real or realistic situation. Second, they require students to apply their knowledge and skill to new situations. By requiring such transfer of student learning, they provide a measure of in-depth understanding, while also reinforcing to learners that a major goal of education is to be able to use what is learned in the wider world beyond the classroom. Third, they naturally integrate 21st-century skills with the big ideas of academic content. They call for genuine applications of thinking (e.g., through creative problem solving), technology use (e.g., to find and critically evaluate information), communication (in writing or other media), collaboration with peers, and habits of mind such as persistence. And, finally, they can recur across grade levels, in increasingly sophisticated forms. For example, whereas elementary school students might be asked to interpret the data on height for their 2nd-grade class and prepare a chart for the 1st-graders that helps them understand how students change from 1 year to the next, high school students can be asked to interpret the data on the spread of the HIN1 infection on each continent over 12 months and prepare a Website, podcast, or newspaper article for a public audience that explains spread rates in relationship to seasonal variation, international travel patterns, and government policies.

The Coalition of Essential Schools (CES), which has long been a leader in promoting more authentic evaluations of students, refers to formal and informal authentic assessments as *performances* (Cushman, 1990). They have outlined in detail the qualities of these performances, drawing on the work of their former research director, Wiggins, mentioned above (see Figure 5.5). For example, in one performance carried out at a CES school, a social studies and science teacher jointly asked students to form teams to investigate different aspects of Latin America's problems of poverty and illiteracy, overcrowding, earthquakes, and political instability. One group had to develop a series of diagrams and maps that showed land movement of the plates of the Earth in Latin America and the cross-section of energy forces below the surface of the land; a second group had to construct and discuss the meaning of maps and diagrams showing the vegetation/climate zones, atmospheric and ocean currents, hydrologic cycle, and important resources of Latin America; and a third group had to construct and explain population maps related to the original migration to and settling of Latin America, the populations living there in 1800–1850, and the different language and racial groups living there today.

While performances often involve an audience or panel from within the school, CES also emphasizes what they call "exhibitions," which are "performance based assessments made visible, public demonstrations of mastery that depend on participation of people from outside the school community as mentors and evaluators" (Davidson, 2007). This public dimension is intended to ensure engagement both within and beyond the school community.

Performance-based assessment does not require that students have individual access to digital media, but it can be greatly enhanced through such one-to-one access. Almost all the laptop programs we observed used performances and exhibitions of this type, as exemplified by the learning expeditions at King. Other examples are found at St. Margaret's Episcopal School in Southern California, a school discussed later in this chapter, where the 7th-grade Life Sciences teacher, Eric Harrington, includes several such performances and exhibitions a year. In 2009–2010, for example, students had to investigate a simulated crime scene and solve the crime by collecting, analyzing, and interpreting samples of blood, hair, bones, and other evidence. Later that year, as part of the QuikSCience competition organized for schools in California and Hawaii, Harrington's students worked in groups to research an environmental issue, conduct a study on it, participate in a community service project, generate a reasonable and feasible solution to the problem, write a report on their findings, and submit their entire project in written and multimedia form to a panel of scientists, educators, business leaders and other judges at the University of Southern California. Two of the school's teams were selected as finalists in the competition to present their findings at USC, with one coming in second place of all participating groups.

FIGURE 5.5. Qualities of Authentic Performances

Structure and Logistics

Typically are public, involving a panel or audience
Involve collaboration with others
Do not rely on arbitrary time constraints

Intellectual Design Features

Are essential, rather than arbitrary or contrived to shake out a grade
Are enabling, designed to direct students to more sophisticated use of
    knowledge and skills
Are complex, contextualized intellectual challenges, not atomized tasks
    with isolated outcomes
Involve students' own research or use of knowledge, not just recall or
    plug-in skills
Are educational and engaging, emphasizing depth more than breadth
Involve ambiguous tasks or problems, rather than ones with one
    known answer

Grading and Scoring Standards

Use criteria to assess essentials, not only easily counted but less
    important errors
Are graded in reference to performance standards, not on a curve
Involve transparent criteria of success that students understand as
    inherent in successful activity
Involve self-assessment as part of the process

Fairness and Equity

Ferret out and identify possible hidden strengths
Minimize needless and demoralizing comparisons
Allow appropriate room for student aptitudes, styles, and interests
Assessment is scaffolded up as necessary, not dumbed down

Source: Summarized from Wiggins (1989)

Standardized Performance Assessment. Although standardized assessments have been designed and implemented ineffectively in the United States, better-designed standardized tests could help us evaluate how
well schools, districts, and states—and the diverse groups of students within them—are progressing toward important educational goals. *Standardized* performance assessments share some of the qualities of the *classroom*

performance assessments described above; however, standardized assessments need to be constructed in a way that allows scoring to be systematically compared across schools, districts, and states. Such assessments
should require both in-depth subject matter and critical analytic ability,
and be amenable to scoring in a standardized fashion by trained readers.

A number of countries and states around the world are using standardized performance assessment in conjunction with classroom performance assessment. In Australia, for example, the state of Victoria offers a
certificate of education for students who successfully complete high school
studies. Successful completion of the certificate requires a combination of
both internal assessment and external assessment. Internal assessment is
conducted via school-assessed course work and tasks, and includes authentic performances such as essays, reports, tests, case studies, products,
and models. External assessment is based on standardized examinations
in each subject area. The exams include both multiple-choice questions
and complex problems or tasks. For example, the 2010 standardized exam
in biology included eight very challenging questions that provided some
background information and put forth a complex task. In one of them,
students had to outline an experiment that would allow them to determine whether the hardness of food pellets provided to animals affects
the balance between energy intake and energy expenditure, including
the hypothesis that would be tested, the experimental procedures, and
the results that would support or negate the student's hypothesis. In another, a student had to refer to time-graphs about incidents of measles at
different points of different years before and after a vaccination campaign,
and of embryonic and fetal organ development throughout pregnancy, to
answer both verbally and graphically a number of open-ended questions
about the spread of the disease, the significance of antibodies, and the
in-utero danger at different periods. In a third question, students had to
examine and consider three distinct mice strains with different amounts
of memory cells, plasma cells, and a specific receptor to explain which
strain would be best at destroying a fast-acting influenza virus and how
blocking the action of the receptor could result in the production of a
more efficient vaccine.

Similarly complex questions are found on the standardized external
assessments for Victoria in other subjects. These questions demand entirely different levels of understanding from the kinds of questions typically
found on standardized assessments in the United States. These complex
questions are more expensive to score than multiple-choice questions,
but can be fairly graded by trained readers with specific rubrics. Other
Australian states, such as New South Wales, are deploying similar types
of questions on their school-leaving examinations.

Given these kinds of assessments, and the kinds of learning challenges they involve, it is no surprise that Australian states are implementing one-to-one technology programs to support more in-depth learning. Victoria rolled out a one-to-one netbook program for all students in 344 middle schools in low-income communities last year. New South Wales has an even larger netbook program covering all high school students in the state.

The approaches that Australia is taking to educational assessment are not unique to that country. Darling-Hammond (2008) reports that most other educationally high-performing nations, including Finland, Sweden, Hong Kong, and New Zealand, also use performance-based assessment.

The United States is behind in this area, but some good work is being done at the state level. For example, the Connecticut Academic Performance Test, which is given to all students beginning in 10th grade and is a requirement for graduation in some districts, provides authentic assessment in reading, writing, math, and science. The reading portion includes a response to literature, in which students must read a short story and then answer open-ended questions as to their reflections, interpretation, connections to other issues, and critical assessment. The writing portion includes two interdisciplinary essays, each of which involves reading two articles on a divisive issue and then writing a three-page persuasive letter on the stance that they take. The math portion involves open-ended questions in which students must answer a question, explain their procedure, show their work, and sometimes draw a visual. And the science section includes an open-response analysis to the results of a lab experiment, as will be further discussed below in the section on formative assessment.

Note that there is not a perfect correlation between performance-based assessment and uses of technology. Connecticut, for example, which does not yet have a statewide laptop program (one was earlier proposed by the governor but not implemented), has gone further in performance-based assessment thus far than has Maine, which does have such a program. Nevertheless, in the long run, the two efforts—to improve assessment by making it more authentic and performance-based, and to improve instruction through better integration and use of digital media—are well aligned. To see why, it is useful to return to the driver's license comparison. If there were only a written test of driving rules, and no actual driving test, there would be no need to incorporate automobiles into driver's training instruction, since students could instead just memorize the book. Similarly, when the predominate assessments we have in many schools are multiple-choice tests, there is little incentive to incorporate powerful digital media in instruction, since the value of that media is to promote more authentic forms of learning that are not yet tested. However, the more we seek to assess students' ability to write meaningful papers, conduct authentic research, analyze scientific data, and solve ill-structured problems, the more value that digital media will have in instruction.

Formative Assessment

Assessment in the United States is too frequently viewed in a punitive, summative manner. Whether through the final exam at the end of a semester or the annual standardized tests, testing is designed to weed out failing students or schools. Yet while there are certainly legitimate reasons for summative assessment, especially if it can be improved as described above, greater benefit comes from formative assessment, which provides feedback to students and teachers that can be used to improve teaching and learning.

The benefits of formative assessment have been demonstrated in both experimental (e.g, Karpicke & Blunt, 2011; Karpicke & Roediger, 2008) and naturalistic research (e.g., Black & Williams, 1998a). In an experiment, for example, Roediger and Karpicke (2006) compared the learning results among two groups of undergraduates, a *study-study group* and a *study-test group*. The study-study group first studied a reading passage, and then restudied it. The second group first studied a reading passage and then completed a test in which they were asked to write down as much of the material from it they could remember. Each group spent the same total amount of time with the material. In the second phase of the study, both groups were tested on the material, also by being asked to write down as much of the material they could remember. This final test took place under three conditions, after a 5-minute, 2-day, and 1-week interval. Interestingly, the study-study group outperformed the study-test group in the first test after 5 minutes. But the study-test group far outperformed the study-study group after 2 days and after 1 week. A second experiment demonstrated that frequent testing was even more valuable, with a study-test-test-test forgetting only 14% of the material after a final test a week later, whereas a study-study-study-test group forgets 28% of the material, and a study-study-study-study work forgets 52% of the material.

Classroom research confirms the tremendous value of formative assessment. Following an exhaustive review, Black and Williams (1998b) conclude that they "know of no other way of raising standards for which such a strong prima facie case can be made" (p. 148). Many of the studies they examined found that the greatest benefits accrue to low-achieving students, who are less able to improve their performance without the kinds of direction that formative assessment provides. Similarly, Reeves (2002) reports that, together with a focus on writing, "frequent assessment with multiple opportunities for improvement" (p. 187) was a key feature of the high-minority, high-poverty, high-achieving schools that he investigated. As he explains,

> The consistent message of the 90/90/90 Schools is that the penalty for poor performance is not a low grade, followed by a forced march to the next unit. Rather, student performance that is less than proficient is followed by multiple opportunities to improve performance. Most of these schools conducted weekly assessments of student progress. It is important to note that these assessments were not district or state tests, but were assessments constructed and administered by classroom teachers. The consequence of students performing badly was not an admonishment to "Wait until next year" but rather the promise that "You can do better next week."
>
> A frequent challenge to this practice is that students should learn to "get it right the first time." The flaw in such a statement is the implied assumption that the traditional "one-shot" assessment is successful in leading students to "get it right the first time." In fact, when students know that there are no additional opportunities to succeed, they frequently take teacher feedback on their performance and stuff it into desks, back packs, and wastebaskets. Students in this scenario are happy with a "D" and unmotivated by an "F." After all, there is nothing that they can do about deficient performance anyway. In a classroom assessment scenario in which there are multiple opportunities to improve, however, the consequence for poor performance is not a bad grade and discouragement, but more work, improved performance, and respect for teacher feedback. In this respect, the use of teacher evaluation based on assessment scoring guides looked much more like active coaching after which improvement was required, and much less like final evaluation from which there was no reprieve. (pp. 188–189)

This kind of learning from feedback features very prominently in the way that youth learn with digital media outside of school. Gee (2003), for example, who has documented 36 learning principles embedded in video games, defines what he calls "the probing principle" as this:

> Learning is a cycle of probing the world (doing something); reflecting in and on this action and, on this basis, forming a hypothesis; reprobing the world to test this hypothesis; and then accepting or rethinking the hypothesis. (pp. 108–109)

Such experiences provide an opportunity for students to test out their hypotheses and then improve their understanding and performance. Our own empirical research on the ways people learn during video games (Rama, 2010) found the probing principle to be the most frequent learning principle exhibited during actual play out of the 36 principles described by Gee.

Further examples of how youth learn from formative assessment can be found from fan fiction sites. On these sites, thousands of youth around the world post original works of fiction based on forms of popular media such as television, movies, books, music, and video games. For example, at one popular site, FanFiction.net, more than 385,000 works have been submitted about Harry Potter books alone, including writing that extends the books, stories that provide alternative endings, and poetry about the books and their characters. One of the most important features of these sites, as revealed by Black's (2008) in-depth study, is the way that youth generously provide and take advantage of feedback to improve their writing. This feedback comes from more than 50,000 beta-reviewers on Fan-Fiction.net who officially sign up to fulfill the role of reviewer, as well as from anyone else who wishes to comment on a particular piece of writing. Black documents the writing improvement among a number of English language learners on FanFiction.net, including one native speaker of Chinese who received more than 6,000 reviews of her writing over a several-year period and used that feedback to steadily craft her writing ability. As Black points out, it is the low-pressure nature of this peer feedback that makes it so valuable and distinguishes it from what usually happens in school, where assessment too often comes in terms of a grade or test score rather than helpful feedback along the way.

Improving Formative Assessment with Digital Media in Schools. Digital media can improve formative assessment in schools through project-work, writing, and computer-based feedback. Project work provides outstanding opportunities for students to get formative feedback, and projects can be organized in a recursive fashion so that students continue to develop competencies and skills over time. An example from Connecticut shows how formative assessment via projects and standardized summative assessment can be tied together. During 9th and 10th grade, high school students complete 10 performance-based activities, made up of two each—one laboratory activity, and one science, technology, and society activity—within five different strands, including energy transformations, chemical structures and properties, global interdependence, cell chemistry and biotechnology, and natural gas energy resources. For example, in the global interdependence strand, a typical laboratory activity is to work with a lab partner to conduct an experiment investigating the effect of acid rain on various building materials to recommend to a town council the best materials for a new statue. The activity involves writing a hypothesis with dependent and independent variables, designing an experiment to solve the problem using a set of suggested materials or others agreed upon, conducting the experiment after approval by the teacher, collecting and organizing data, and communicating the findings in a laboratory report including a statement of the problem, a description of the experiment, experimental data, conclusions, and analysis of reliability and validity. The science portion of the standardized Connecticut Academic Performance Test then refers back to one of the 10 performance-based activities students have carried out and asks open-ended questions that relate to its context. In 2010, for example, students taking the statewide test were provided with (1) the set of procedures that one student group had used for the acid rain lab experiment and (2) the results that it found; the test-takers were then asked to identify the problem that the student group was investigating in its experiment and to describe two things the group could do to increase confidence in its results.

Almost all the one-to-one schools we have studied use extensive project work with formative feedback as part of their instructional cycle. For example, at the Engineering Academy, a key motivation for redesigning the 9th- through 11th-grade curriculum, as described earlier in this chapter, was to allow a more iterative unfolding of projects over a 3-year period, so students could learn from their earlier project work and continually improve their products.

Digital media can also be used to enhance self-assessment during projects. For example, at Howard Middle School (pseudonym) in Maine, students design and build model bridges out of wood and then place a brick on top of the bridge while videotaping. Most of the bridges hold the brick, but for those that don't, a subsequent frame-by-frame analysis of how and where the bridge collapsed indicates to the students the precise flaws in their design. At the same school, French language students perform 3–4 skits throughout the year, incorporating the French vocabulary and themes they are studying in class, and the skits are videotaped by other students. Afterward, the performers view the videos and fill out a reflection sheet on their language use, looking in particular for language structures that have been the focus of instruction, and then work on improving their language use for the future.

Use of digital media can also facilitate formative feedback on student writing. Writing becomes much more visible and readable when performed digitally than by hand. This makes possible more feedback from peers, who can read (and thus respond to) their classmates' writing more easily from a screen or a printout than from a handwritten paper. Some of the schools we have investigated, such as King Middle School, make the appointment of student editors and the use of peer feedback central components of the writing process.

Digital writing also promotes more feedback from teachers, again due in part to the easier readability of digital material. For example, a teacher we interviewed in Maine told us that she could read and respond to students' essays printed out from a computer at about three times the speed that she could read and respond to handwritten papers. Teachers are increasingly foregoing even printing out student writing, or requiring students to do so, and commenting on material either right at students' screens or via online communication—through blogs, e-mail, or Google Docs, or in special online writing environments. In our observations, we noted that teachers who respond to work at students' screens or via digital communication tend to provide more frequent feedback than those who only respond to work that is written down or printed out, and students we interviewed indicate that this more frequent feedback is quite helpful.

Also, as discussed throughout this book, writing digitally allows learners to more easily share their writing outside the classroom—for example, through blogs. Even in cases where feedback provided from people outside the classroom is minimal, the very act of writing for real readers appears to help students better focus on the audience and purpose of their written work, an important step in becoming a good writer.

A number of the districts with laptop programs use commercial automated writing evaluation programs, such as My Access or Writing Roadmap, to try to provide more frequent feedback to students on their writing. Automated scores on a 4-point or 6-point scale are provided by software, which compares countable syntactic, semantic, and discourse features of essays to a corpus of other essays on the same topic previously written by students in the same grade level and scored by human readers. These programs typically also provide both word-level editorial suggestions (somewhat like a souped-up version of Microsoft Word's spelling and grammar check) and narrative feedback on the overall writing style. The latter is sometimes given in a generic form; for example, in My Access, a 6th-grader who gets a 4 out of 6 on a persuasive essay will get the same narrative feedback as any other student of the same grade with the same score on the same genre. Finally, these programs come with an array of other features bundled within a general online writing environment, such as rubrics, word banks, and sample essays for students; mechanisms for teachers to comment digitally on student work; and a system for archiving, managing, and analyzing individual and class portfolios. We have investigated and written about these systems extensively previously, and our most recent observations confirm what we concluded before—that the tools themselves have flaws in their ability to provide accurate scores and feedback, but they can have some utility as classroom management tools and motivators for students to revise their work, depending on how the software is used (see, e.g., Grimes & Warschauer, 2010). Opinions on the value of the software vary from school to school and teacher to teacher. A number of the elementary teachers we interviewed felt the feedback and editorial tools were too complex for their students to take advantage of, and preferred other uses of computers that emphasized writing for authentic audiences. This was especially true of elementary school teachers that had a lot of English learners. In general, we found that enthusiasm among elementary school teachers for automated writing evaluation programs fell over time, whereas enthusiasm for public writing through blogs and other online forums tended to stay strong, but, again, this differed from school to school and teacher to teacher. Measurable gains in writing outcomes that we found in Saugus, where all classes had access to both blogs and the My Access program, were consistent across the district and did not significantly vary depending on how much teachers used one tool or the other. We thus could not differentiate how much the different types of activities (writing on My Access or writing on blogs and wikis) contributed to improved writing outcomes. However, due to the cost of My Access and the mixed opinions about it among teachers, the district stopped purchasing the program districtwide after the grant ended, leaving the decision for further purchase and use to individual schools.

Finally, technology-rich classrooms provide opportunities for students to learn from other types of computer-based feedback when they engage with interactive software programs, games, or online quizzes. For example, teachers in several schools we visited have used SpellingCity, an online program available in both free and commercial versions that allows the teaching and testing of vocabulary and spelling while potentially saving teacher time in correction. Earlier in this book, we pointed out that tutorial-based learning has not proven very successful in schools, and we remain convinced that it should not be the principle way that computers are integrated into instruction. However, our observations in classrooms suggest that the use of tutorials, skill-based games, and quizzes can be beneficial if used on an occasional basis at the point of need, such as commonly occurs in laptop classrooms.

Problems with the U.S. approach to assessment are gradually gaining more attention among national policymakers. Recently, the U.S. Department of Education has indicated its intention to change some of the assessment policies of No Child Left Behind. Specifically, the Department has signaled its desire to move away from the current approach, which only considers the percentage of students who meet proficiency standards, to a more sophisticated approach that takes into account all students' year-to-year progress. And the Department has also funded two national consortia to develop assessments for reading and math that can better measure complex skills and provide more formative information to students, parents, and teachers (U.S. Department of Education, 2010).

Although these initiatives will take time to bear fruit, and they are far from a complete solution, they are at least steps in the direction of measuring what we truly value rather than valuing what we can most easily measure.

COMBINING CURRICULUM, PEDAGOGY, AND ASSESSMENT: UNDERSTANDING BY DESIGN

Although in this chapter we have discussed curriculum, pedagogy, and assessment sequentially, they are obviously highly integrated. Good teachers and schools, with or without laptops, consider their major curricular goals and then plan assessments and instruction accordingly.

There is one particularly interesting framework for combining the three called *understanding by design*. This framework was originally developed by Wiggins and McTighe (1998), discussed earlier in this chapter for their work on assessment, and later incorporated into a broader educational reform approach called *schooling by design* (2007). McTighe and Seif (2010) have then elaborated how this approach can specifically be implemented to support 21st-century learning.

Understanding by design is based on a "backward planning" model in which teachers first identify the *big ideas* or *enduring understandings* that they want students to get out of a course (or, in the more updated version, the combination of big ideas and 21st-century skills) and the *essential questions* that these ideas entail. The next step is to develop the appropriate assessments that will enable teachers to determine the extent to which students have understood these big ideas and essential questions, and then the scope and sequence of learning activities with these ideas, questions, and assessments in mind.

Many of the schools in our study used this kind of approach. For example, the teams of teachers at King Middle followed a comparable model in designing their learning expeditions. One school we have been investigating, St. Margaret's Episcopal School in Southern California, has used the Wiggins/McTighe understanding by design framework more explicitly and provides an interesting example of the integration of curriculum, pedagogy, and assessment in a technology-rich environment.

St. Margaret's is a pre-K–12 private school in a suburban area of Orange County, California. Although most students at the school tend to do very well academically and enter college, school leaders want to be sure that they are promoting the kinds of deep understanding, interdisciplinary thinking, autonomous learning, media and communications skills, and leadership ability needed to excel in academia and society. In 2007, they thus launched an educational reform process based on two frameworks, understanding by design and 21st-century learning. The reform started in St. Margaret's middle school and is gradually being extended to the high school and elementary school. Technology is viewed as an important tool for this process, and most classrooms in the school offer one-to-one access to netbooks or laptops.

We have conducted case studies of a number of middle school teachers at St. Margaret's who have been involved in this educational reform, and earlier in this chapter provided examples of the life science teachers' learning projects. An in-depth look at another teacher, Rian Otto, illustrates the understanding by design process in a technology-rich classroom. Otto teaches multiple sections of a 6th-grade social studies class at St. Margaret's called World Cultures. She teaches in a netbook classroom with a cart of Dell computers, wireless Internet access, and other tools such as a digital whiteboard.

Otto began the 2009–2010 school year by developing three enduring understandings, three essential questions, and three broad learning goals for her World Cultures classes for the year (see Figure 5.6).

As a next step, she developed enduring understandings, essential questions, and content and course skills for each unit of the course that corresponded to the above but were particularized for the unit. Figure 5.7 indicates the understandings, questions, and skills for a unit titled "Understanding Archaeology and the Dawn of Civilization."

Otto then developed summative and formative measures to assess whether students had developed the understandings and skills she had chosen. For example, in the unit on archaeology and the dawn of civilization, there were four main summative assessments: (1) a team project to develop a model/drawing of a museum exhibit about hominids, (2) a written diary from the point of view of one of several people (e.g., farmer, mother, child, artisan, trader, religious leader) living in the Catal Huyuk settlement 8,000 years ago, (3) an interview for an archaeology position, and (4) a vocabulary test. Formative assessments built toward these, and included, for example, development of a résumé for an archaeology position, responses to questions about unit content on an online discussion forum, and development of a unit vocabulary chart.

Teaching and learning activities were then developed with unit goals and assessments in mind. In this particular unit, activities included exploring a Website about the discovery of a prehistoric skeleton, video-conferencing with an archaeologist, participating in oral and computer-mediated discussions on the course topics, playing vocabulary *Jeopardy!* and writing vocabulary poems, and completing a jigsaw activity in which each member of a group had to contribute a different piece of informa-

FIGURE 5.6. World Cultures Class Understandings, Questions, and Learning Goals (Academic Year)

Enduring Understandings	Essential Questions	Learning Goals
The study and interpretation of the past can help us examine and understand the present, shape the choices we make, and predict future events.	How am I connected to the people in the past and what lessons can I learn from them that will influence my future?	Encourage students to become interested in learning about the past and help them to understand the importance of history and how it relates to their lives today.
Different cultures, no matter how far removed through time or distance, impact each other.	How does the environment shape human activity? How does human activity shape the environment?	Teach students how to learn, with an emphasis on study strategies, note-taking skills, active reading techniques, research and writing skills, organization, and time management.
Civilizations succeed or fail based upon cooperation and conflict among people, the effects of geography, the acts of an individual or group, and achievement of humankind.	What is the impact of cultural interaction on individual cultures and the rest of the world?	Create a classroom atmosphere of cooperative interaction and mutual respect.

tion about prehistoric humans from an online search. There was also time devoted to group work on the development of the museum exhibit.

This unit occurred early in the year. Several of the approaches used were repeated later in the year on a more sophisticated level. For example, in a subsequent unit on ancient Egypt, instead of simply writing a diary from the point of view of individual characters, they instead wrote a screenplay that incorporated specific facts and inferences about government, education, religion, and agriculture.

Otto is a talented and successful teacher. Yet she is just one of many teachers we have observed who are able to leverage technology to promote better learning through authentic projects. In all these cases, as in Otto's classroom, the key is not the technology itself, nor project work

FIGURE 5.7. World Cultures Class Understandings, Questions, and Skills (Unit on Understanding Archaeology and the Dawn of Civilization)

Understandings	Essential Questions	Content Skills	Course Skills
Historians and archaeologists employ a variety of tools to investigate the past and interpret its story.

Humankind developed in a series of stages over millions of years.

People of the Old Stone Age developed technologies to feed, clothe, and shelter themselves. Art and language became important new tools for people to communicate ideas and beliefs.

In the New Stone Age, agriculture led to the development of communities and civilizations. These early civilizations established a system of government, maintained a stable food supply, specialized labor, developed culture, and traded with others. | How am I connected to the people in the past and what lessons can I learn from them that will influence my future?

Whose story is it? How should we evaluate historical information in order to understand a more complete and fair picture of the past?

What skills and tools are most essential for survival?

Which development from the Old Stone Age or New Stone Age was most critical in helping to form civilizations? | Define and use in context a provided list of unit vocabulary words.

Interpret data using a timeline.

Explain what advantages primary sources have over secondary sources.

Identify methods and tools that archaeologists use.

Explain how early humans adapted to and modified their environment to survive.

Identify the ways in which agriculture changed human life.

Identify and analyze the components of a civilization: agriculture, specialization, education, religion, government. | Vocabulary recognition and usage

Reflective writing

Research

Public speaking

Interpretation/ analysis/ synthesis

Analytical and creative writing: ideas and content, sentence fluency, organization and conventions |

itself, but the combination of project work with digital media and (1) a curriculum focused on deep understanding, (2) a pedagogy that combines direct instruction and mentoring to promote student-centered learning, and (3) classroom assessments that are both performative and formative.

VIRTUAL SCHOOLING

One other educational design for digital learning that has received much attention lately is that of virtual schooling—in other words, education that takes place online or via computer software. Several recent books argue that transition to virtual schooling is necessary to solve educational problems (Christensen, Horn, & Johnson, 2008; Moe & Chubb, 2009; Peterson, 2010). Most recently, a policy organization led by former Florida governor Jeb Bush presented a framework to accelerate such a transition (Digital Learning Council, 2010).

There are ideas worth heeding in these works. As the Digital Learning Council (2010) argues, we should be providing digital devices to all learners and streamlining textbook adoption procedures to facilitate the use of digital texts. It is also certainly the case, as all these works argue, that customization of learning is a powerful affordance of digital media, and one that should be better exploited. Finally, extant virtual schools do provide a valuable service by making available courses that students wouldn't ordinarily be able to take, either because their neighborhood schools don't offer them or because the students are homebound.

Yet, the three books listed above go beyond arguing that we might expand and improve virtual schooling, a point that is well taken. Rather, they argue that we should look to virtual schooling as a wholesale solution to educational problems—in other words, that virtual instruction should not merely complement in-person teacher instruction but should replace it on a large scale. Christensen, Horn, and Johnson (2008), for example, suggest that 80% of high school instruction will be conducted online by 2024, a change they claim would be welcome.

The authors of these works present a variety of scenarios for virtual schooling. It can be conducted either with an online instructor or via computer software, and it can take place either at home or in restructured schools, where in-person instructors would play a reduced advisory role. The argument for massive transition to virtual schooling rests on two claims that are made in each of the above three books. First, it is argued that the cost of education needs to be brought under control and that this can only be accomplished by dramatically reducing the number of teachers. Second, the books claim that such a reduction of the teaching workforce will be beneficial since virtual education is supposedly much more student-centric and effective than classroom education.

The first of these arguments is based on the work of economists Baumol and Bowen (1966), whose seminal study explained why in-person services inevitably rise in cost compared to other products and services that can be automated. Since the amount of labor to produce a basket of goods has fallen dramatically over time due to mechanization, the relative cost of labor for in-person services, whether in education, health care, or the performing arts, will thus necessarily go up. This is indeed true, and helps explain why education and health care costs are steadily going up as a percentage of total spending not only in the United States, but also in other industrialized countries (Baumol, 1996). However, as Baumol (1996) explains, nations that become more productive can afford to spend increasing amounts on education and health care, precisely because of the falling costs of other goods and services, so there should be no need to take drastic cost-reduction measures. To put it in perspective, the relative cost of receiving other in-person services, such as getting a haircut or eating in a restaurant, has also increased over time, but people have not stopped those activities due to the rise in price.

The argument that online or computer-delivered instruction would improve learning similarly falls back on the discussion generated by Baumol's work. Baumol (1996) pointed out that performing artists got around the rising costs of their labor by shifting from live concerts to high-fidelity recorded work, thus providing individual listeners a listening experience of equal or higher quality without having to pay for expensive concert tickets. Supporters of virtual schooling suggest that the same thing can happen with education, that we can provide learners a higher-quality learning experience by direct contact with digital material without the mediation of a teacher (Christensen, Horn, & Johnson, 2008; Moe & Chubb, 2009; Peterson, 2010). And they support their argument with positive examples of online learning to date.

However, education is a much more interactive process than listening to music, and one that benefits a great deal from in-person instruction. Online learning can be effective for learners with a high degree of literacy, motivation, and autonomy, but is generally not successful for learners who are lacking in these areas and who are plentiful in public schools (Barbour & Reeves, 2009). That's because face-to-face communication has powerful affordances compared to online communication. In-person communication is more fast-paced and flexible than online communication, as it allows for the quick interpretation of gestures, facial expressions, and other audiovisual clues from dozens of people simultaneously as well as the quick and easy reference to drawings, charts, or physical artifacts. This rich human and physical environment of a classroom usually allows students to better follow what a teacher is saying, and also allows a teacher to quickly diagnose how students are following a presentation and thus make rapid adjustments to get a point across better. A warm smile or even a pat on the back from the teacher provides important affective support. A teacher can also rapidly break a class into pairs, small groups, or large groups, and easily have students move around the room to show each other their work and discuss ideas. While all these types of interaction can be simulated via computer, those computer-based interactions generally take more time and are not as rich in communicative content.

These comparative benefits of face-to-face interaction were seen in the network science study discussed earlier in this chapter. As Feldman and colleagues (2000) state in their conclusion to the study,

> The experience of the network science curricula to date has led us to doubt that virtual communities for K to 12 students can replace classroom-based communities. Our reservations are based on how difficult it has proved to get substantive discussions going among participating classrooms. These reservations have been reinforced by our analysis of class discussions. . . . Given the timing, monitoring, nuanced voice, eye contact, and on-the-spot decision making required to engage students in reflective discussions, online discussions are a poor substitute by comparison. Most simply, the necessary subtleties of face-to-face interaction have no sufficient analogue online. It would be especially unfortunate if, in our ardent attempts to help classrooms get online discussions going, we inadvertently undermined efforts to improve the quality of class discussions. (p. 97)

In addition, many types of powerful experiential learning, such as the robotics competition at Dos Pueblos High, can't be duplicated at all in an online environment. The value of face-to-face interaction and collaboration helps explain why, 30 years after the invention of the Internet, centers of innovation are still highly concentrated in small geographic clusters, such as Silicon Valley, Bangalore, and Tel Aviv. It also explains why the best universities feature in-person instruction, while online colleges are noted more for their cost savings or ability to reach working adults rather than for their high quality of instruction.

A massive transition to virtual schooling could have a particularly negative impact on low-performing students who often lack the independent orientation toward learning, intrinsic motivation, time management skills, literacy, and technology skills required for success in virtual learning environments. There is already a high attrition rate in virtual schools (Barbour & Reeves, 2009), but students at least have the opportunity to drift back to the regular classroom. Where will they drift back to when their regular classes no longer exist? It is for these reasons that even some supporters of virtual schools recognize that they will lead to increased inequality (see, e.g., Peterson, 2010). That is not a desirable direction for our country.

Florida has demonstrated some of the benefits of targeted virtual education, with the highly touted Florida Virtual School extending opportunity to many homeschooled youth or others desiring online classes (Peterson, 2010). However, as seen in a recent exposé, the dark side of virtual schooling is also on display in the state, with students in Miami-Dade County now being placed into teacherless online classes against their will (Herrera, 2011). When students report to class, a "facilitator" assigns them to work at a computer. The new system was put in place not to improve instruction but to save money, since virtual classes in Florida, unlike classes with teachers, have no maximum class sizes. Indeed, an administrator admitted to the *New York Times* that even if students were struggling, mandatory virtual instruction was necessary since "there's no way to beat the class-size mandate without it." One parent said that her "jaw dropped" when she found out that her daughter was assigned to a virtual rather than an actual Spanish class; the student had previously taken online Spanish by choice but did not want to do so again. Another student, who herself chose to be in a virtual class, spoke out for the other 35 to 40 students in her room who were forced into a teacherless class. "None of them want to be there," said the girl, "and for virtual education you have to be really self-motivated. This was not something they chose to do, and it's a really bad situation to be put in because it is not your choice" (Herrera, 2011).

Of course, as highlighted throughout this book, computer-mediated communication and online learning can have powerful affordances for learning, including customizing instruction for individual students, putting students in contact with a wide range of people and resources, and presenting digital simulations and assessments. There are undoubtedly many situations in which students will better grasp material presented via computer than in person due to the ability to stop and repeat a video, carry out an interactive task, or receive rapid feedback. However, face-to-face interaction offers many forms of support as well, and the withdrawal of those supports can be hazardous, especially for low-performing students. It is precisely because of the differential affordances of face-to-face and computer-mediated communication that online interaction should complement rather than replace in-person interaction, so that the benefits of both can be combined.

Christensen, Horn, and Johnson (2008) argue that interactive software can be developed to replace teachers, but the examples of technology-enhanced learning they point to in their book, such as the innovative California charter school, High Tech High, and the game-based New York City public secondary school, Quest to Learn, undermine rather than support that point. Neither of these well-funded schools is substituting online or computerized instruction for in-person teachers. On the contrary, both feature low student-teacher ratios and extensive opportunities for teachers' professional development and collaborative planning, with teachers leading small groups of students in the kinds of hands-on project work discussed throughout this book (Neumann, 2009; Salen, Torres, Wolozin, Rufo-Tepper, & Shapiro, 2011). At Quest to Learn (2011), for example, project work is typically carried out with 10 to 12 students working with one teacher, a ratio under half that of the average class in New York City's other public secondary schools, "to ensure that each student's needs are closely monitored by faculty" (p. 1). This contradiction in Christensen, Horn, and Johnson's book is illustrative of the difference between learning *via* computers and learning *with* computers. While their book calls for a massive transition to learning *via* computers, through online- and software-based instruction to *reduce the need for teachers*, these positive examples they point to involve learning *with* computers, where successful integration of technology into instruction *requires highly skilled teachers*.

Surveys of both parents and the general public suggest that "opposition to earning some credits online may be softening, but opposition to earning most high school credits online is growing stronger" (Rose & Gallup, 2007, p. 39). The public is right. The objective of broadening educational choice through offering some courses online should not detract from our commitment to building effective schools with the infrastructure, leadership, and skilled teaching force needed for educational improvement. How to build and maintain these learning environments is the topic of the next chapter.

6

Environments

Technology is a process, not a thing.

—Nik Honeysett (2008)

Developing and sustaining a successful educational environment with digital media is partly a matter of selecting the right tools, but more importantly involves a process of constructing the relationships that allow these tools to be maintained, replaced, repaired, and deployed in instruction and assessment. All these things are elements of a *sociotechnical infrastructure*, which includes both a network of tools as well as the relationships that allow tools to be exploited for desired ends (Jewett & Kling, 1991; Lee, Dourish, & Mark, 2006; Star & Ruhleder, 1996).

Some of the technical elements of such an infrastructure have been discussed in Chapter 3. In this chapter, we first discuss two different approaches for providing individual devices to students, and then examine the role of leadership and teacher development in high-quality high-tech schools.

DEVICES: PROVIDED BY SCHOOLS OR "BYOT"?

The most common model of educational laptop programs involves provision of equipment by the school or district. This has many advantages, including assurance of a uniformity of device, and control of the equipment for maintenance and software updates by the school. With prices of devices steadily falling, such a solution will become more affordable over time, especially if systematic changes are made so that the full-cost savings are taken into account. For example, provision of one-to-one computers can result in less photocopying, less purchase of bubble sheets for assessments, replacement of printed texts with less expensive (or free) digital ones, decommissioning of computer labs and thus better use of room space, or more funding from the state due to small increases in average daily attendance. A study by Project RED (2010) found that the projected savings of a one-to-one program from these and other areas come to $448 per student year, which is much more than enough to purchase and maintain individual netbooks, laptops, or media tablets for students. Unfortunately, though, our systems are such that some of these items come from separate budgets and the potential cost savings of an educational technology program are thus not immediately realizable to the schools or districts that must purchase devices. For that reason, many districts find one-to-one programs unaffordable.

The One Laptop per Child program works on another model, in which devices are provided to children, but the families are partially or wholly responsible for maintaining them. This model has generally not worked well, in that machines break down and are not repaired. In Uruguay, for example, where there is a national OLPC program, surveys suggested that more than 100,000 out of the country's 400,000 laptops were out of commission less than 2 years into the program, with the highest degree of unusable computers in the poorest areas of the country (see Warschauer & Ames, 2010).

An alternative model is for parents to purchase the devices themselves. This is often carried out in voluntary laptop programs, either in private schools or occasionally in public schools. A number of the school districts we have investigated have had such voluntary programs, with parents having the ability to either opt in or opt out if they could not or did not wish to purchase a device (see discussion in Warschauer, 2006). These programs work in a variety of ways. Some are bring-your-own-technology, or BYOT, programs, in which the families purchase either whatever laptops they want or one of a restricted set of laptops. In other cases, the schools select a device and software combination that parents then lease to own. These programs leverage parent resources but at a great disadvantage in that they restrict children's participation based on their parents' willingness and ability to buy in.

Districts that wish to better leverage family resources but still provide equitable access to all children are thus considering some kind of modified BYOT program in which parents are encouraged to buy a device for their children, but schools will provide one in case parents do not. Such a program still has difficult parameters to work out, such as the following:

1. What models of device are prescribed for students? A particular laptop brand? Any laptop? Or any Internet-connected digital device? Or a range of laptops or devices that meet particular specifications?

Greater flexibility will suit the needs of families, who may already have a device available or who wish to purchase a particular brand, but flexibility can make implementation more complicated in the classroom if students' hardware and software differ dramatically.

2.   For families who opt out of purchasing, do their children only get to use the school-provided device at school, or can they take it home in an unrestricted fashion? Or something in between (e.g., only taking it home if the parents purchase insurance, or only taking it home weekdays but not weekends or on a special checkout basis)?

Allowing students to take devices home in an unrestricted manner provides the greatest equity, but is also most costly, both because it provides disincentives for parents to purchase devices and also because of the greater likelihood of damage in an out-of-school environment.

3.   Is there any means-testing? Can all parents opt out, or must they state or prove low income? Or are there different ways to opt out, with, for example, children whose families opt out due to low income receiving a device that can be taken home, but with children whose families opt out for other reasons only receiving a device that can be used in schools?

For simplicity's sake and to maintain the broadest base of support, means-testing should probably be avoided.

4.   What about school or district wireless access? Is there sufficient bandwidth both for uploading and downloading for a one-to-one program? And are security settings in place to handle a wide range of devices?

Some districts develop two types of networks, one for school-provided equipment and one for BYOT.

5.   How else can the district support students who may not have home access to computers or the Internet for completing assignments?

Schools may need to consider extending the hours of their libraries or media labs to give students additional opportunities for completing homework and other assignments. Districts can also partner with local companies to encourage discounts to parents who purchase computers or Internet access.

An example of a BYOT program in Ohio is discussed later in this chapter. First we review other elements of a successful sociotechnical infrastructure.

LEADERSHIP

The Texas Technology Immersion Project represents one of the largest and most rigorous studies of laptop programs in the United States to date.

A group of 21 grade 6 to 8 middle schools that carried out an immersion program with laptops was studied in depth and compared to a control group of 21 schools of matched demographics. The study found many positive results, including the following:

- Immersion teachers grew in technology proficiency, their use of technology for professional productivity, their use of technology for student learning activities, and their support for learner-centered instruction at significantly faster rates than control teachers.
- Students at immersion schools had fewer disciplinary actions than control-group students, became significantly more proficient in technology, and experienced more intellectually demanding work.
- Students in the immersion schools experienced larger gains than control-group students in both math and reading and for both advantaged and disadvantaged students at all three times a comparison was made, i.e., in 7th grade after 2 years of the immersion program, in 8th grade after 3 years of the program, and in 9th grade after students had already exited the program (Texas Center for Educational Research, 2009).

However, program implementation and results were not uniform across the 21 schools. Students at schools that achieved the broadest implementation—specifically, schools that kept laptops in students' hands and encouraged the use of laptops at school and at home for academic pursuits—earned the highest test scores. And a key factor in laptop implementation was leadership. Teachers in each of the immersion schools were surveyed to indicate the extent to which their administration demonstrated leadership by establishing a clear vision and expectations, encouraging integration of technology in instruction, providing needed supports and resources, and involving staff in decision making about technology.

Based on survey results, a "leadership index" was established, as well as an "implementation index" that took into account factors such as teachers' technology integration, use of learner-centered instruction, and use of technology for communication and professional productivity, as well as students' access to and use of technology for learning activities. Not surprisingly, there was a strong relationship between the leadership index and the implementation index, in addition to, as mentioned above, the relationship between implementation and improved test scores.

The results of the Texas project provide quantitative evidence to confirm what we have witnessed in our observations across the country, that strong administrative leadership is critical to the success of school technology programs. Leadership comes in many different levels in educational technology programs. Sometimes political leadership is key, when an executive articulates a compelling vision of why and how to bring about educational reform, as accomplished by Governor Angus King in Maine to launch that state's laptop program. More frequently, it comes from school district leaders, including superintendents, assistant superintendents, and information or instructional technology directors. In many districts, IT and instructional technology leaders are separated by a wide gap, with only the latter concerned about educational issues and the former attending only to technical matters. Yet when IT directors also have a broad educational vision, such as that demonstrated by Jim Klein in Saugus or Dan Maas in Littleton, they can contribute a great deal to educational reform with technology. At the school level, leadership emerges from innovative principles, such as Mike McCarthy at King Middle, who has twice been named Middle School Principal of the Year in Maine, as well as from teachers who rise from the ranks to leadership, such as Amir Abo-Shaeer at the Dos Pueblos Engineering Academy or David Grant, who coordinates technology integration strategy at King. But in almost all cases, strong educational reform programs with technology stem from strong leadership.

What, then, does leadership entail? Our research in schools, and the experiences of others (see, e.g., K–12 Computing Blueprint, 2010), suggests that five leadership steps are vital to success.

First, it is critical to develop a strong overall vision of what educational reform with technology can achieve and how it can be brought about. For extensive reforms carried out at the district or statewide level, it is often helpful to bring together a task force to help create and articulate that vision. For example, the groundbreaking Maine Learning and Technology Initiative was launched following the development of a detailed report (Task Force on the Maine Learning Technology Endowment, 2001) from a statewide task force.

Second, all relevant stakeholders need to be identified and involved in the planning and implementation of a program. These include board of education members, district and school administrators, staff from relevant departments (curriculum, instruction, assessment, information technology, instructional technology), teachers, students, parents, and local civic and business leaders. Special emphasis needs to be put on ensuring teacher participation, involvement, and buy-in.

Third, detailed plans need to be developed that delineate specific objectives, identify a pathway to their achievement, lay out evaluation procedures along the way, and consider long-term funding and sustenance of the project. Since successful educational reform projects involve a changing of the culture of schools, as well as development of the curricula, assessments, and other elements to facilitate such a change, they are most successful when carried out gradually over a multi-year period, rather than through attempts at sudden imposition. Phases of an educational technology program thus might include development of an initial plan, initial professional development, implementation and evaluation of a pilot program, and gradual extension of the reform to additional grade levels over a multi-year period.

Fourth, there need to be ongoing opportunities for professional development of teachers and collaborative planning among them, with an emphasis on transforming teaching and learning, not just on how to use tools. (This is such an important point that it will be elaborated in more detail in the following section.)

Fifth, ongoing communication with all stakeholders is required. Partly, this can take place online through keeping district and school Websites updated with project information, videos, and copies of evaluation reports. The use of social media such as blogs, wikis, and Twitter can also help keep stakeholders informed and allow them to participate in ongoing dialogue. Public events to report on the program's developments and to showcase successes—including, for example, exhibition of outstanding student projects—are also very helpful for maintaining positive momentum for reform.

Before turning to an example of how these elements are put in place, we consider at more length the role of the most critical actor in educational reform, the teacher.

TEACHERS

Larry Cuban (1986), one of the foremost historians of U.S. education, used historical documents and records to study the history of technology integration in U.S. schools, dating back to the 19th century, and covering technologies such as radio, film, and television. Cuban found that a similar pattern has existed throughout this history, regardless of the technology involved. First, great enthusiasm would be shown about a new technology's potential to transform teaching and learning, with industry leaders and the press marveling about how it would revolutionize instruction. Then, a small demonstration project would be introduced under ideal conditions and with very supportive and prepared teachers, yielding, in these idealized conditions, excellent technology integration and outcomes. Next would come a top-down effort, often with the support of industry but with little involvement or feedback from teachers, to impose the technology on a larger scale. When imposed broadly in this manner, teachers would largely ignore the technology; it would only marginally be used in instruction and have little overall impact on how students learn. Finally, people would blame teachers as either being too conservative, lazy, or stupid to master and integrate the technology, and momentum for technology-enhanced reform would die out—at least until the next miracle technology appeared years later. Cuban (2001) thinks a similar cycle is now happening with computers, which he believes are destined to sit largely unused in the corners of classrooms like televisions or film projectors.

Evidence suggests that on this last point, Cuban is wrong. In large numbers of districts and schools across the country, computers and the Internet have already achieved a level of classroom use far exceeding that ever reached by radio, film, or television. And all indications are that use of computers in schools will continue to grow. The reasons why are obvious. Internet-connected computers have an entirely different connection to knowledge production than radio, film, or television ever did. A typical knowledge worker spends all day on a computer for work, without a television, radio, or film projector at all, and if students are to learn to produce knowledge, they require access to networked digital devices as well.

Having said that, Cuban is right that there are important challenges in integrating technology in instruction, so it is important to study how these can be overcome. Becker (2000a), speaking directly to the issues Cuban raised, used national surveys to identify what factors contribute to teachers' use of technology in schools. He concluded that teachers make substantive use of technology under three conditions, all of which are achievable.

First, Becker found that teachers who had fewer computers in their classroom tended to use them less than teachers who had more computers in their classroom. He also found that the availability of computers in the classroom was more important for promoting frequent use than the availability of computers in laboratories. In this regard, we can take a lesson from industry. Computers were introduced into businesses as early as the 1950s, but they had an effect on productivity only decades later, once they became ubiquitous in offices. Employees increased their productivity when they had daily individual access to computers much more than when they used computers on an occasional or shared basis. Research suggests that the trends that Becker found earlier—with more access to computers leading to more use—continue in today's laptop era, with classrooms with regular one-to-one access to laptops featuring more use and better integration of technology than classrooms that share access to laptops through mobile carts (Russell, Bebell, & Higgins, 2004). With the price of digital devices continuing to fall, a steady increase in access to technology in the classroom is taking place, and this condition is gradually being met.

Becker found that teachers' expertise and comfort in using computers professionally was the second critical factor. Part of this expertise depends on technical skills in computer operation, but part of it relies on the broader skill set suggested by the TPACK framework discussed earlier. Simply put, teachers who have expertise and comfort in using technology to achieve specific pedagogical aims in particular content areas will be much more likely to integrate digital media in instruction.

Third, Becker found that teachers' general beliefs and values about how children learn influenced how much they used computers in the classroom. Teachers who most frequently and productively used computers in instruction were those who, according to survey responses, were "not very comfortable with a transmission-oriented pedagogy" (p. 10) but instead embraced an alternative philosophy of education that included two pedagogical emphases:

1. attending to the "meaningfulness" of instructional content for each student—for example, by developing examples connected to students' own personal experience or by providing opportunities for students to present detailed explanations of their reasoning; and
2. developing students' capacities to understand a subject deeply enough, and see the interrelationships of different ideas and issues, so they are able to know how and when to apply their knowledge to particular contexts and communicate their understandings to others. (pp. 10–11)

Of the three factors Becker pointed to, teacher beliefs are probably the most difficult to change, since they are molded by decades of societal experiences. Cuban's historical work, both on the history of educational technology as well on broader reform processes in education (see, e.g. Cuban, 1993), points to the great power of norms in influencing teachers' values, beliefs, and practices. Cuban suggests that deeply held cultural beliefs about the nature of knowledge, how teaching should occur, and how children should learn steer policymakers and teachers toward certain forms of instruction, and that these forms of instruction are guided by the broader role of the schools to "inculcate into children the prevailing social norms, values, and behaviors that will prepare them for economic, social, and political participation in the larger culture" (Cuban, 1993, p. 249). These norms are deeply embedded in teachers, who learn them from their own experiences as schoolchildren, and thus, without a change in norms, tend to teach the way they were taught.

Changing patterns of teaching thus involves changing norms and beliefs. To a certain extent, those norms reflect our national values, and

FIGURE 6.1. Five Strategies for Professional Development in One-to-One Environments

- Engage Teachers' TPACK
- Engage Teachers in Project-Based Inquiry
- Engage Teachers in a New Global Skill Set
- Engage Teachers in Performance-Based Assessment
- Engage Teachers in Professional Learning Communities and Networks

Source: Spires, Wiebe, Young, Hollebrands, & Lee (2009)

thus depend on national action. Probably the best way to start changing norms of teaching would be to change norms of standardized assessment, as suggested in the previous chapter. Norms and beliefs can also be influenced at the district, school, and individual level. But that does not happen overnight, which is why attempts at sudden change will result in disappointment. Rather, as has been demonstrated in research going back 15 years (Sandholtz, Ringstaff, & Dwyer, 1997), learning to use technology well is a multi-year process, and involves not only the development of teachers' technical skill, but also an evolution of their ideas about teaching and learning.

What, then, can be done to help ensure that this process of teacher development is successful and that teachers do successfully integrate technology in instruction? Based on prior research and theory and lessons from their professional development experiences, a team of researchers from North Carolina State University has articulated five key strategies for professional development for teachers in one-to-one computing environments (see Figure 6.1; Spires et al., 2009):

The first strategy is to *engage teachers' TPACK*. Professional development related to technology too often focuses only on technological skills (how to operate the hardware or the software) or on technological-pedagogical knowledge (how to use a tool for generic instruction). However, knowledge of the interaction between technology, pedagogy, and content is critical to the successful use of new media. Professional development thus needs, to the extent possible, to be content-driven and to focus on instruction in particular areas of math, science, social studies, language arts, and other subjects.

A second strategy is to *engage teachers in project-based inquiry*. The essential elements of project-based learning include considering ideas and posing questions; gathering and analyzing information; creatively synthesizing information and solving problems; evaluating and revising results; and sharing, publishing, and/or acting on what was learned (Spires et al., 2009). Teachers will be able to best carry out project-based inquiry in the classroom when they have directly experienced it in professional development. As Spires and colleagues explain,

> Teachers must immerse themselves in the project-based inquiry process in order to understand how to develop the skill set that involves facilitation, coaching, improvisation, and consultation. Likewise, teachers must engage in authentic intellectual work in order to grasp the multi-layered facets of what is involved in creating comparable learning conditions for their students. (p. 16)

A third strategy is to *engage teachers in a new global skill set*. Teachers need to understand key outcome goals discussed earlier in the book, such as expert thinking, complex communication, and adaptive expertise. These goals are all consistent with project-based learning, but do not necessarily flow from it; after all, it is entirely possible to design projects that do not require or promote much expert thinking or complex communication. These skills should be the focus of both the project work that teachers themselves carry out during professional development and that which they plan for their students during professional development.

A fourth strategy is to *engage teachers in performance-based assessment*. The need for such assessment was elaborated at length in the previous chapter. However, many teachers have little experience with this kind of assessment and will need a good deal of collective practice to successfully design such assessments.

The fifth strategy is to engage teachers in *professional learning communities and networks*. Teachers are among the most isolated groups of professionals, carrying out almost all their work individually in their own classrooms. Yet the kinds of educational reform discussed in this book require teachers to collaborate with, and learn from, other teachers at their school and beyond. Unfortunately, the structure of the school day as organized in U.S. schools usually provides little time for collaboration. The best laptop schools that we have observed have had an alternative structure in which teachers have opportunities for frequent meetings and collaboration (Warschauer, 2006). Principals should do their best to make professional collaboration possible within the constraints of their particular system. Opportunities and environments for online collaboration should be introduced as well in districts, both in general and tied to particular professional development efforts. Teachers should also be introduced to a wide range of online tools for engaging with broader networks of educators for ongoing professional learning.

Finally, many of the above strategies can be strengthened by having a technology facilitator on site, whether a full-time staff person, a regular teacher who has some facilitation responsibilities, or someone from another school or district office who visits the site regularly. This helps ensure that teachers have access to just-in-time mentoring that is most beneficial to them (Cron & Osborne, 2009).

Littleton Public Schools, discussed throughout this book, provided an outstanding example of implementation of these professional development strategies. Using funds from federal programs, foundation support, and grants, it offers 7 full days of workshops each summer for teachers in its Inspired Writing professional development programs. A weeklong program early in the summer (for new teachers in the program) includes 2 days on the writing curriculum, 1 day on the technologies involved, and 2 more days on how to implement the curriculum with the tools. Two less structured days at the end of summer, for both new and returning teachers to the program, involve a combination of refresher training and team planning time. The district's chief information officer, Dan Maas, reports that the professional development has become much more effective now that it is task-oriented rather than technology-oriented (e.g., focusing on how to do peer review with wikis, rather than focusing on wikis) and subject-specific (i.e., language arts) rather than general. This summer training is complemented by visits to schools throughout the year by district trainers, who co-teach innovative lessons with teachers on request. Through these efforts, the district has worked to establish what Maas calls "beachheads" in every school of one or more teachers who "really know how to use 21st-century tools in the writing process" and can provide models or support for colleagues (e-mail interview, December 2010). Our survey of Littleton teachers found that more than three out of four rated their own ability to integrate technology in instruction as high, an impressive result that likely contributed to the positive learning outcomes in the district discussed earlier. The district has also introduced the TPACK model to principals in sessions on assessing the work of Inspired Writing classrooms.

In summary, Larry Cuban is right—there are powerful norms that influence teacher behavior, and the transition to effective use of technology in schools is neither immediate nor easy. However, the experiences of Littleton and other districts (see, e.g., Maddux, Gibson, & Diodge, 2010; Sandholtz et al., 1997) suggest that the strategies discussed above can successfully change teachers' practices to better foster learning with new media.

AN EXAMPLE FROM OHIO

Forest Hills School District is a 7,800-student district in Cincinnati, Ohio, with a "bring your own laptop" program (McCrea, 2010). The development and implementation of the program and of the district's broader educational technology efforts are illustrative of a number of the issues discussed in this chapter related to sociotechnical infrastructure, including BYOT, leadership, and professional development.

Cary Harrod, the district's instructional technology specialist, explained to me that the roots of the BYOT program go back 5 years, when a teacher training initiative began. Over a 5-year period, almost all teachers in the district were provided a tablet PC and wireless projector and involved in a 1-year professional development program for better integration of technology in teaching. The professional development took place through monthly face-to-face meetings and ongoing online collaboration. Through the professional development, teachers learned about new Web-based tools, used them for their own development, and explored ways they could be used in instruction.

During this same period, to promote better leadership for educational reform with technology in the district, Harrod and about 50 other Forest Hills teachers and staff participated in an action-research-based professional development program called Powerful Learning Practice (PLP), which involves attendance at in-person workshops, access to 21st-century curriculum "Webinars," and immersion in an asynchronous virtual community by teams of five educators from a school together with a select group of experienced PLP Fellows. The PLP program is designed to help teams of educators develop their understanding of the transformative potential of emerging technologies and how they can be realized and sustained in classrooms and schools.

Harrod participated in the PLP program for 3 years, 2 of which were spent as a fellow, providing her an extensive background and support network both inside and outside the district for leading innovative technology programs.

Over this 5-year period, the district continually sought to implement a one-to-one laptop program, but could not obtain sufficient funding to launch and sustain such an initiative. As an interim step, mobile laptop carts were installed in schools, so teachers could at least provide students individual laptops on a scheduled basis, and a district-wide wireless network was put in place as well.

In 2010, the district decided to launch a "bring your own laptop" program as a way to make more technology available in the classroom in an era of slashed budgets. The program's name, Partnership for Powerful Learning, communicates two key emphases: (1) that technology should be deployed to create better and more powerful learning experiences, and (2) that a close partnership between teachers, parents, children, and the community was necessary to ensure success.

Partnership for Powerful Learning began with a pilot program in January 2011 among 7th-grade students at Nagel Middle School (the one middle school in the district). Since almost all Nagel teachers had already participated in the district's 1-year professional development program on new technology, and the principal and a small group of teachers had additionally completed the year-long PLP program, the school was well positioned to take leadership in this initiative.

At the time of this writing, the program is in its first semester of implementation. A second district wireless network has been established to accommodate student-owned devices. Seventh-grade students are allowed to bring any netbook PC, notebook PC, tablet PC, Mac Pro, or iPad to school, as long as the device does not have 3G capacity (since 3G access would enable students to bypass district Internet filters). The district partnered with a local vendor to offer special pricing on certain netbook, notebook, and tablet models, but families can instead use other devices they already have or purchase one someplace else. The existing 130 district-owned laptops for 7th-graders, which had been previously available on laptop carts for teachers to borrow, are still available for teachers to use to supplement laptops provided by students.

A total of 356 students are bringing their own laptops to school in this first semester of implementation. Although the program in the short run does not provide full one-to-one access—since the 356 students who bring laptops combined with the 130 district-owned laptops does not yet equal the 550 7th-grade students in the district—it still has several advantages, according to Harrod. First, the program benefits students who bring their own laptops, including a number of students with compelling reasons for doing so due to disabilities. Second, even students who do not bring their own laptops benefit from much greater access, since the district's 130 laptops can be shared among the approximately 200 students who don't bring their own computers rather than among all 550 7th-grade students in the district. Third, teachers are easily able to set up one-to-one environments when most needed, again because the number of computers available to be checked out is spread among far fewer students. The program's guidelines make clear that anytime laptops are required for learning, they are to be brought into the classroom and made available to students who do not have their own.

A number of other steps have been taken to develop and maintain a strong sociotechnical infrastructure for the Forest Hills project. An online environment for learning has been established using Google Apps, Edublogs, and Schoology, a combined social networking and learning management platform; teachers had been using these or other similar tools in their professional development programs previously. Parents' input and support has been carefully nurtured. A series of parent meetings and a Website for the program keeps families informed. Parent responses to an early survey both indicated sufficient support to launch the program, with a majority of those responding indicating that they would send devices to school with their children, and, equally important, raised questions that the program needed to address, such as how laptops would be kept secure, what educational value the program would bring, and how issues of possible inequity could be addressed. Harrod explained that these questions helped the district sharpen and clarify its objectives and policies for the program. Later, a parental advisory council was formed, which meets 1–2 times a month in person and holds ongoing online discussions to ensure that parents' voices are continually included.

Equal attention has been paid to preparing students for participation in the program. All students who intended to bring their own devices were required to first go through a 3-hour session on a Friday afternoon or Saturday that covered program goals and policies, and introduced social media that would be used in instruction. Students who did not intend to bring their own devices were invited to these events as well.

Most important, teacher capacity and interest in the program have been cultivated throughout. Teachers' input was sought early on through a series of meetings and a survey in which 95% of those who responded expressed support for launching the program. Even prior to the implementation, teachers at the school collaborated in five-person planning teams that teach the same group of students, an organizational setup that assisted close coordination among teachers in planning and carrying out the initiative. A new year-long professional development program was implemented at Nagel covering topics such as developing a professional learning community; promoting 21st-century knowledge and skills; understanding the characteristics of a 21st-century learning environment; and re-envisioning learning with TPACK, project-based learning, understanding by design, and alternative assessment. Finally, an innovative process of evaluation has been established, in a partnership between the district leadership, classroom teachers, and a University of Cincinnati professor, Carla Johnson. The entire pilot project is being viewed as an action-research project to examine the following questions:

1. How has the world changed, and what does this mean for education?
2. How is 21st-century learning different from learning in the 20th century and what does it look like?
3. What is high-quality teaching and learning?
4. What does the classroom look like in the 21st century?
5. What supports are necessary for teachers and students to grow in an increasingly digital world?

One of the five-teacher 7th-grade teams that is especially interested in these questions is collaborating with the university professor to collect and analyze classroom data to address them. Individual teachers from other teams have been invited to participate in the action-research project as well.

Surveys have been taken of teachers, parents, and students about the program, with the initial response very positive. The action-research findings are being combined with survey data and other information to assess whether the program should go forward, and, if so, how. Tentative plans are to extend the project to 8th through 12th grades in coming years. Future plans also include raising additional funds from the community to offer more district-owned devices to students who lack them, considering offering a leasing option to parents, and assessing whether the range of devices allowed should be broadened.

7

Conclusion

Technology—no matter how well designed—is only a magnifier of human intent and capacity. It is not a substitute.

—Kentaro Toyama (2010)

We began this book by contrasting the implementation process and results of a school laptop program in Littleton, Colorado, with that of the One Laptop per Child program carried out in Birmingham, Alabama. We can now summarize the many elements of implementation in Littleton that made that program a success (see Figure 7.1).

Virtually all these elements were absent in the Birmingham laptop program, due not to negligence but to design. The OLPC program that Birmingham followed, at least as articulated by OLPC founder and spokesperson Nicholas Negroponte, eschews efforts to improve curriculum, assessment, and pedagogy as either too time-consuming or simply unnecessary, since Negroponte (2009, 2010) believes that children can teach not only themselves but also their parents simply by having access to an XO laptop. Those local OLPC implementations that have followed Negroponte's advice have had predictably negative results (see discussion in Warschauer & Ames, 2010).

Negroponte's approach can be summarized as trying to improve learning without improving teaching. Beyond the somewhat unique Birmingham context, his utopian approach is unlikely to get much of a hearing in U.S. school districts. However, there is another vision of educational reform with technology emerging that on the surface has very different motivations and principles than OLPC but similarly seeks to decouple improved learning from improved teaching. That vision seeks to reduce the number of teachers and limit their role through a shift to virtual schooling, with teachers either instructing large numbers of students in online classes or simply offering occasional assistance to students who principally learn through computer-based tutorials. But although online learning has

FIGURE 7.1. Key Elements of Littleton Laptop Program

Goals	Improving learning outcomes and equity by a technology-enhanced educational reform program
Vision and Planning	A 25-page report outlining the district's educational technology and information literacy vision and plan
Curriculum	University Literacy Framework and Writer's Workshop
Pedagogy	Use of Web 2.0 tools to promote authentic writing
Student Assessment	Formative and summative assessment through writing benchmarks
Technological Infrastructure	Wireless access in all schools; a laptop model carefully chosen for program needs that performed well
Online Environment	Use of Google Apps, blogs, and wikis
Professional Development	Seven days of workshops focused on curriculum and TPACK and co-teaching opportunities with technology integration specialists
Staged Rollout	A year-long pilot program in Year 1, extension to three grade levels in Year 2, and extension to three more grade levels in Year 3
Program Evaluation	Benchmarks and methods set based on standardized tests, writing assessments, demonstrations of student work, site observations, technology literacy measures, and interviews with graduates

a role to play in education, a massive transition to virtual schools would only hamper education, as demonstrated by the high attrition rate of students in virtual schools and such schools' lack of ability to recruit and meet the needs of low-performing students (Barbour & Reeves, 2009).

The fact is that technology itself does not bring about reform, but instead tends to amplify extant beliefs and practices (Toyama, 2010; Warschauer, 1999, 2000; Warschauer et al., 2004). Teachers, schools, and educational systems built on the notion that students learn best from tutorial learning, drill and practice activities, development of isolated skills, and multiple-choice testing will simply find ways to use technology to carry out these kinds of practices more efficiently, perhaps at a distance. Similarly, teachers, schools, and educational systems devoted to promoting in-depth learning through authentic projects and performance-based assessment will deploy technology to amplify those practices as well.

The use of digital media to reform education is a challenging process. I have sometimes wondered whether we should seek less complicated paths to education improvement. Education, though, is a complex undertaking, any way that you look at it—from the intricate cognitive processes of the human mind to the systemic complexities of human capital development in the 21st century. In this context, more simplistic approaches to educational reform—for example, by replacing teachers with computers or by punishing schools and teachers for their students' multiple-choice test results—cannot meet the challenges at hand.

Educational reform with digital media is not an effort that will be completed in 5, 10, or 20 years. After all, we have been learning how to do schooling with books and paper for centuries and have still not gotten it right. Those who write off attempts to improve schools with technology based on imperfections to date are shortsighted. With society, technology, and schools constantly evolving, we are in the early stages of what will be a very long process.

Although the effort required is great, so are the potential rewards. Digital media provide the most powerful tools for communication, analysis, and research that have ever existed in human history. We are experiencing a revolution in the means of production of knowledge greater than any since the development and diffusion of the printing press (Harnad, 1991). As educators, we thus have an important and exciting opportunity—to remake our schools to best take advantage of these powerful new media so as to prepare students for successful participation in a rapidly changing world. Our test, as it were, consists of two intertwined questions: What is the role of information technology in schools, and what is the role of schools in an information society?

Take out your laptops, netbooks, or tablets, and begin composing your response to these questions. You can use any information you find on the Internet, from your professional learning community, or from your personal learning network. Your answer may take the form of an interdisciplinary curriculum, experiential pedagogy, performance-based assessment, or innovative infrastructure design. You may express your answer via an essay, film, app, or three-dimensional knowledge map. You have a lifetime to respond.

References

Aesop. (1909). The two crabs [fable]. In *The Harvard Classics, Volume 17, Part I*. New York: P. F. Collier & Son.

Atkinson, R. D., & Andes, S. M. (2009). *The Atlantic century: Benchmarking EU & U.S. Innovation and Competitiveness*. Washington, DC: Information Technology and Innovation Foundation.

Attewell, P., & Battle, J. (1999). Home computers and school performance. *The Information Society, 15*(1), 1–10.

Attewell, P., & Winston, H. (2003). Children of the digital divide. In P. Attewell & N. M. Seel (Eds.), *Disadvantaged teens and computer technologies* (pp. 117–136). Münster, Germany: Waxmann.

Augustine, N. R., Barrett, C., Cassell, G., Grasmick, N., Holliday Jr., C., Jackson, S. A. et al. (2010). *Rising above the gathering storm, revisited: Rapidly approaching category 5*. Washington, DC: The National Academies Press. Retrieved May 23, 2011, from http://www.nap.edu/openbook.php?record_id=12999&page=R1

Baldi, S., Jin, Y., Skemer, M., Green, P. J., Herget, D., & Xie, H. (2007). *Highlights from PISA 2006: Performance of U.S. 15-year-old students in science and mathematics literacy in an international context*. Washington, DC: National Center for Education Statistics.

Barbour, M. K., & Reeves, T. C. (2009). The reality of virtual schools: A review of the literature. *Computers & Education, 52*, 402–416.

Barron, B., Martin, C. K., Takeuchi, L., & Fithian, R. (2009). Parents as learning partners in the development of technological fluency. *International Journal of Learning and Media, 1*(2), 55–77.

Barron, B., Walter, S., Martin, C. K., & Schatz, C. (2010). Predictors of creative computing participation and profiles of experience in two Silicon Valley middle schools. *Computers & Education, 54*(1), 178–189.

Bascomb, N. (2011). *The new cool: A visionary teacher, his FIRST Robotics team, and the ultimate battle of smarts*. New York: Crown.

Baumol, W. J. (1996). Children of performing arts, the economic dilemma: The climbing costs of health care and education. *Journal of cultural economics, 20*(3), 183–206.

Baumol, W. J., & Bowen, W. G. (1966). *Performing arts: The economic dilemma*. New York: The Twentieth Century Fund.

Becker, H. J. (2000a). Findings from the Teaching, Learning, and Computing survey: Is Larry Cuban right? *Educational Policy Analysis Archives, 8*(51). Retrieved March 23, 2011 from http://epaa.asu.edu/epaa/v8n51/

Becker, H. J. (2000b). Who's wired and who's not?: Children's access to and use of computer technology. *The future of children, 10*(2), 44–75.

Birmingham News Editorial Board. (2010). Our view: It's no laughing matter that Birmingham Superintendent Craig Witherspoon has a whole lot on his hands and a school board that doesn't really get it. Retrieved December 17, 2010, from http://blog.al.com/birmingham-news-commentary/2010/11/our_view_its_no_laughing_matte_1.html

Black, P., & Wiliam, D. (1998a). Assessment and classroom learning. *Assessment in education, 5*(1), 7–74.

Black, P., & Wiliam, D. (1998b). Inside the black box: Raising standards through classroom assessment. *Phi Delta Kappan, 80*(2), 139–148.

Black, R. W. (2008). *Adolescents and online fan fiction.* New York: Peter Lang.

Bork, A. (1985). *Personal computers for education.* New York: Harper & Row.

Bransford, J., Mosborg, S., Copland, M. A., Honig, M. A., Nelson, H. G., Gawel, D., et al. (2009). Adaptive people and adaptive systems: Issues of learning and design. In A. Hargreaves, A. Lieberman, M. Fllan, & D. Hopkins (Eds.), *Second International Handbook of Educational Change* (pp. 825–856). Dordrecht, NL: Springer.

Brennan, K., Monroy-Hernández, A., & Resnick, M. (2010). Making projects, making friends: Online community as catalyst for interactive media creation. *New Directions for Youth Development, 128,* 75–83.

Bureau of Labor Statistics. (2008). The 30 fastest growing occupations covered in the 2008–2009 Occupational Handbook. Retrieved August 5, 2008, from http://www.bls.gov/news.release/ooh.t01.htm

Calkins, L. (1994). *The art of teaching writing.* Portsmouth, NH: Heinemann.

Capps, R. (2009). The good enough revolution: When cheap and simple is just fine. *Wired, 17*(09). Retrieved March 23, 2011 from http://www.wired.com/gadgets/miscellaneous/magazine/17-09/ff_goodenough

Castells, M. (1998). *End of millennium.* Malden, MA: Blackwell.

Chall, J. S., & Jacobs, V. A. (2003). The classic study on poor children's fourth-grade slump. *American Educator, Spring.* Retrieved March 23, 2011 from http://www.aft.org/newspubs/periodicals/ae/spring2003/hirschsbclassic.cfm

Christensen, C. M., Horn, M. B., & Johnson, C. W. (2008). *Disrupting class.* New York: McGraw-Hill.

Clark, D. B., Touchman, S., & Skjerping, C. (2009). Increasing access for English language learners in online learning environments: Integrating Spanish and English audo and text language supports to support science learning. Paper presented at the Annual Meeting of the American Educational Research Association, San Diego.

Cohen, M., & Miyake, N. (1986). A worldwide intercultural network: Exploring electronic messaging for instruction. *Instruction Science, 15,* 257–273. doi:10.1007/BF00139614

Common Core. (2010). A challenge to the partnership for 21st century skills. Retrieved November 29, 2010, from http://www.commoncore.org/p21-challenge.php

Cron, J., & Osborne, J. (2009). *Mid-year evaluation report on the progress of the North Carolina 1:1 learning technology initiative.* Raleigh, NC: Friday Institute for Educational Innovation, North Carolina State University.

Crowe, C. (2009, November 26). A costly lesson: A look at Birmingham's curious commitment to the XO laptop. *Black & White.* Retrieved March 23, 2011 from http://www.bwcitypaper.com/Articles-i-2009-11-26-232786.113121_A_Costly_Lesson.html

Cuban, L. (1986). *Teachers and machines: The classroom use of technology since 1920.* New York: Teachers College Press.

Cuban, L. (1993). *How teachers taught: Constancy and change in American classrooms 1890–1980.* New York: Longman.

Cuban, L. (2001). *Oversold and underused: Computers in classrooms, 1980–2000.* Cambridge: Harvard University Press.

Culp, K. M., Honey, M., & Mandinach, E. (2005). A retrospective on twenty years of education technology policy. *Journal of Educational Computing Research, 32*(3).

Curtis, M., Williams, B., Norris, C., O'Leary, D., & Soloway, E. (2003). *Palm handheld computers: A complete resource for classroom teachers.* Eugene, OR: International Society for Technology in Education.

Cushman, K. (1990). Performance and exhibitions: The demonstration of mastery. Retrieved December 1, 2010, from http://www.essentialschools.org/resources/123

Darling-Hammond, L. (2008). Performance-based assessment: An international perspective. [Video] Paper presented at the Forum for Education and Democracy. Retrieved November 22, 2010, from http://www.youtube.com/watch?v=WpTT_ewXmKI

Davidson, J. (2007). Exhibitions: Demonstrations of mastery in essential schools. Retrieved December 1, 2010, from http://www.essentialschools.org/resources/237

DeBell, M., & Chapman, C. (2006). *Computer and Internet use of by students in 2003.* Washington DC: National Center for Education Statistics.

de Castell, S., & Luke, A. (1986). Models of literacy in North American schools: Social and historical conditions and consequences. In S. de Castell, A. Luke, & K. Egan (Eds.), *Literacy, society, and schooling* (pp. 87–109). New York: Cambridge University Press.

Digital Learning Council. (2010). *Digital learning now!* Tallahassee, FL: Foundation for Excellence in Education. Retrieved March 23, 2011, from http://www.excelined.org/Docs/Digital%20Learning%20Now%20Report%20FINAL.pdf

Drew, C. (2011, January 7). Rethinking Advanced Placement. *New York Times.* Retrieved March 23, 2011, from http://www.nytimes.com/2011/01/09/education/edlife/09ap-t.html

Dynarski, M., Agodini, R., Heaviside, S., Novak, T., Carey, N., Campuzano, L. et al. (2007). *Effectiveness of reading and mathematics software products: Findings from the first student cohort.* Washington, DC: U.S. Department of Education.

Education Initiatives. (2010). Retrieved March 23, 2011, from http://www.birminghamal.gov/pdf/education.pdf

Feldman, A., Konold, C., & Coulter, B. (2000). *Network science, a decade later: The Internet and classroom learning.* Malwah, NJ: Lawrence Erlbaum Associates.

Fitzhenry, R. I. (Ed.) (1993). *The Harper book of quotations,* 3rd ed. New York: HarperCollins.

Gabriel, A. R. (2010). Inspiring education. *EdTech: Focus on K–12, April–May.* Retrieved March 23, 2011, from http://www.edtechmag.com/k12/issues/april-may-2010/inspiring-education.html

Gee, J. P. (2003). *What video games have to teach us about learning and literacy.* New York: Palgrave Macmillan.

Gee, J. P. (2004). *Situated language and learning: A critique of traditional schooling.* New York: Routledge.

Giacquinta, J. B., Bauer, J. A., & Levin, J. E. (1993). *Beyond technology's promise: An examination of children's educational computing at home.* Cambridge, UK: Cambridge University Press.

Glaser, R. (1984). Education and thinking: The role of knowledge. *American Psychologist, 39*(2), 93–104.

Goode, J., Estrella, R., & Margolis, J. (2006). Lost in translation: Gender and high school computer science. In J. M. Cohoon & W. Apray (Eds.), *Women and information technology: Research on underrepresentation* (pp. 89–114). Cambridge, MA: MIT Press.

Gray, L., Thomas, N., & Lewis, L. (2010a). *Educational technology in U.S. public schools: Fall 2008.* Washington, DC: National Center for Education Statistics.

Gray, L., Thomas, N., & Lewis, L. (2010b). *Teachers' use of educational technology in U.S. public schools: 2009 (NCES 2010-040).* Washington DC: National Center for Education Statitics, Institue of Education Sciences, U.S. Department of Education.

Greaves, T. W., & Hayes, J. (2008). *American's digital schools 2008: The six trends to watch.* Encinitas, CA: Greaves Group and Hayes Connection.

Grimes, D., & Warschauer, M. (2010). Utility in a fallible tool: A multi-site case study of automated writing evaluation. *Journal of Technology, Language, and Assessment, 8*(6), 1–43.

Harnad, S. (1991). Post-Gutenberg galaxy: The fourth revolution in the means of production and knowledge. *Public-Access Computer Systems Review, 2*(1), 39–53.

Harrison, G. (2002). Any road. On *Brainwashed* [CD]. Dark Horse/EMI. (2002).

Hatano, G., & Oura, Y. (2003). Commentary: Reconceptualizing school learning using insight from expertise research. *Educational Researcher, 32*(8), 26–29.

Herrera, L. (2011, January 17). In Florida, virtual classrooms with no teachers. *New York Times.* Retrieved March 23, 2011, from http://www.nytimes.com/2011/01/18/education/18classrooms.html

Honeysett, N. (2008). Good project gone bad: Planning, managing and delivering complex technology projects. Paper presented at the American Association of Museums Annual Conference, Denver. Retrieved December 13, 2010, from http://www.mediaandtechnology.org/downloads/Good_Gone_Bad-Honeysett.pdf

Ito, M., Baumer, S., Bittanti, M., boyd, d., Cody, R., Herr-Stephenson, B. et al. (2009). *Hanging out, messing around, geeking out: Living and learning with new media.* Cambridge, MA: MIT Press.

Ito, M., Horst, H., Bittanti, M., boyd, d., Herr-Stepheson, B., Lange, P. G. et al. (2008). Living and learning with new media: Summary of findings from the digital youth project. Retrieved December 22, 2008, from http://digitalyouth.ischool.berkeley.edu/files/report/digitalyouth-WhitePaper.pdf

Jenkins, H. (2009). *Confronting the challenges of participatory culture: Media education for the 21st century.* Cambridge, MA: MIT Press. Retrieved March 23, 2011, from http://mitpress.mit.edu/books/chapters/Confronting_the_Challenges.pdf

Jewett, T., & Kling, R. (1991). The dynamics of computerization in a social science research team: A case study of infrastructure, strategies, and skills. *Social Science Computer Review, 9,* 246–275.

K–12 Computing Blueprint. (2010). Leadership. Retrieved November 25, 2010, from http://www.k12blueprint.com/k12/blueprint/leadership.php

Kafai, Y. B., Peppler, K., & Chapman, R. (2009). *The Computer Clubhouse: Constructionism and creativity in youth communities.* New York: Teachers College Press.

Karpicke, J. D., & Blunt, J. R. (2011). Retrieval practice produced more learning than elaborative studying with concept mapping. *Science Express.* Retrieved March 23, 2011, from http://www.sciencemag.org/

Karpicke, J. D., & Roediger III, H. L. (2008). The critical importance of retrieval for learning. *Science, 319,* 916–968. doi:10.1126/science.1152408

Kay, A. C. (1991). Computers, networks and education. *Scientific American, 265*(3), 138–148.

King Middle School Expeditionary Learning Planning Group. (2009). Expeditionary Learning at King Middle School. Retrieved March 23, 2011, from king.portlandschools.org/files/onexpedition/resources/elatkms.pdf

Klein, J. (2010). Linux on netbooks. Retrieved December 21, 2010, from http://community.saugususd.org/swattec/page/Linux+on+Netbooks

Kling, R. (1999). What is social informatics and why does it matter? *D-Lib Magazine December 15, 2001, 5*(1). Retrieved March 23, 2011, from http://www.dlib.org/dlib/january99/kling/01kling.html

Kling, R. (2000). Learning about information technologies and social change: The contribution of social informatics. *The Information Society, 16*(3), 1–36.

Kling, R., & Lamb, R. (2001). IT and organizational change in digital economies: A sociotechnical approach. In E. Brynjolfsson & B. Kahin (Eds.), *Understanding the digital economy: Data, tools, and research* (pp. 295–324). Cambridge, MA: MIT Press.

Koehler, M. J., & Mishra, P. (2010). Technological pedagogical content knowledge (TPACK). Retrieved December 21, 2010, from http://tpack.org/

Kraemer, K. L., Dedrick, J., & Sharma, P. (2009). One laptop per child: Vision vs. reality. *Communications of the ACM, 52*(6), 66–73. doi:10.1145/1516046.1516063

Kulik, J. A. (2003). *Effects of using instructional technology in elementary and secondary schools: What controlled evaluation studies say.* Arlington, VA: SRI.

Landsberg, M., & Rathi, R. (2005, May 5). Elite school will expel AP classes. *Los Angeles Times*, p. B1.

Lave, J., & Wenger, E. (1991). *Situated learning: Legitimate peripheral participation.* Cambridge, UK: Cambridge University Press.

Lee, C. P., Dourish, P., & Mark, G. (2006). *The human infrastructure of cyberinfrastructure.* Proceedings of CSCW '06. Retrieved March 23, 2011 from http://portal.acm.org/

Legionzero. (2009). [Untitled comment on blog.] Retrieved September 28, 2010, from http://www.olpcnews.com/countries/uruguay/a_steep_cost_or_a_profitable_i.html

Lehman, C. (2010). Chris Lehman, Science Leadership Academy, speaks at TED. Retrieved November 29, 2010, from http://21k12blog.net/2010/06/05/chris-lehmann-science-leadership-academy-speaks-at-ted/

Lenhart, A., Ling, R., Campbell, S., & Purcell, K. (2010). Teens and mobile phones. Retrieved May 25, 2010, from http://www.pewinternet.org/

Levy, F., & Murnane, R. J. (2004). *The new division of labor: How computers are creating the next job market.* Princeton, NJ: Princeton University Press.

Littleton Public Schools. (2008). Littleton Public Schools Universal Literacy Framework. Retrieved September 29, 2010, from http://www.littletonpublicschools.net/Portals/0/ITS/Technology/Universal-Literacy-Framework.doc

Littleton Public Schools. (2009). A premier education: Educational technology and information literacy plan. Retrieved May 2010, from http://www.littletonpublicschools.net/Portals/0/ITS/Technology/Final-ETIL-Plan-2009-2012.pdf

Llosa, L., & Slayton, J. (2009). Using program evaluation to improve the education of young English language learners in US schools. *Language Teaching Research, 13*(1), 35–54.

Lupita. (2009). Blog comment, Writing with laptops. Retrieved September 29, 2010, from http://bit.ly/cxXbAn

Maddux, D. D., Gibson, D., & Diodge, B. (Eds.). (2010). *Research highlights in technology and teacher education 2010.* Chesapeake, VA: Society for Information Technology & Teacher Education.

Margolis, J., Estrella, R., Goode, J., Holme, J. J., & Nao, K. (2008). *Stuck in the shallow end: Education, race, and computing.* Cambridge, MA: MIT Press.

Martin, T., & Schwartz, D. L. (2005). Physically distributed learning: Adapting and reinterpreting physical environments in the development of fraction concepts. *Cognitive Science, 29,* 587–625.

McCrea, B. (2010). Bring your own technology. Retrieved November 24, 2010, from http://thejournal.com/articles/2010/08/05/bring-your-own-technology.aspx

McQuillan, J. (1998). *The literacy crisis: False claims, real solutions.* Portsmouth, NH: Heinemann.

McTighe, J., & Seif, E. (2010). An implementation framework to support 21st century skills. In J. Bellanca & R. Brandt (Eds.), *21st century skills: Rethinking how students learn* (pp. 149–171). Bloomington, IN: Solution Tree Press.

Mishra, P., & Koehler, M. J. (2006). Technological pedagogical content knowledge: A framework for teacher knowledge. *Teachers College Record, 108*(6), 1017–1054.

Moe, T. M., & Chubb, J. E. (2009). Liberating learning: Technology, politics, and the future of education.

National Assessment of Educational Progress. (2010). The Nation's Report Card. Retrieved October 27, 2010, from http://nationsreportcard.gov/ushistory_2010/

National Commission on Writing. (2004). *Writing: A ticket to work or a ticket out.* New York: The College Entrance Examination Board.

National Research Council. (2000). *How people learn: Brain, mind, experience, and school.* Washington DC: National Academy Press.

Negroponte, N. (2009). Lessons learned and future challenges. Presentation at the Reinventing the Classroom: Social and Educational Impact of Information and Communication Technologies in Education Forum, Washington, DC, September. Retrieved September 12, 2010, from http://www.olpctalks.com/nicholas_negroponte/nicholas_negroponte_lessons_learned_and_future_challenges.html

Negroponte, N. (2010). Comments at the Techonomy Conference, What Technology Wants vs. What People Want Panel, Lake Tahoe, CA, August. Retrieved December 13, 2010, from http://www.youtube.com/watch?v=2rz2yhkahM0

Neuman, S. B., & Celano, D. (2006). The knowledge gap: Implications of leveling the playing field for low-income and middle-income children. *Reading Research Quarterly, 41*(2), 176–201.

Neumann, R. (2009). Charter schools and innoviation: The High Tech High model. *American Secondary Education, 36*(3), 51–69.

Newell, A., & Simon, H. A. (1972). *Human problem solving.* Englewood Cliffs, NJ: Prentice-Hall.

NSF Task Force on Cyberlearning. (2008). *Fostering learning in the networked world: The cyberlearning opportunity and challenge.* Washington, DC: National Science Foundation.

Orfield, G., Losen, D. J., Wald, J., & Swanson, C. (2004). *Losing our future: How minority youth are being left behind by the graduation rate crisis.* Cambridge, MA: The Civil Rights Project at Harvard University.

Papert, S. (1993). *The children's machine: Rethinking school in the age of the computer.* New York: Basic Books.

Paris, S. (2005). Re-interpreting the development of reading skills. *Reading Research Quarterly, 40*(2), 184–202.

Partnership for 21st Century Skills. (2010). Framework for 21st century learning. Retrieved November 29, 2010, from http://www.p21.org

Peppler, K., & Kafai, Y. (2007). From SuperGoo to Scratch: Exploring digital media production in informal learning. *Learning, Media, and Technology, 32*(2), 149–166.

Peppler, K., & Warschauer, M. (2009, April). Lessons from Brandy: Creative media production by a child with cognitive (dis)abilities. Paper presented at the Annual Meeting of the American Educational Research Association, San Diego.

Peterson, P. E. (2010). *Saving schools: From Horace Mann to virtual learning.* Cambridge, MA: Belknap Press of Harvard University Press.

Pfaffman, J. (2007). It's time to consider open source software. *TechTrends, 51*(3), 38–43.

Project RED. (2010). Project RED key findings. Retrieved March 23, 2011 from http://www.one-to-oneinstitute.org/pdf/Project%20RED%20Key%20Findings.pdf

Quest to Learn. (2011). Quest to Learn frequently answered questions. Retrieved January 3, 2011, from http://q2l.org/kits/parentkit/Q2L_FAQs.pdf

Rama, P. (2010). Video games and learning. Poster presented at the Science Technology Engineering Math (STEM) Summit, Irvine, CA, February.

Ravitch, D. (2010). *The death and life of the great American school system.* New York: Baic Books.

Reeves, D. (2002). *Accountability in action.* Denver, CO: Advanced Learning Press.

Rideout, V., Foehr, U. G., & Roberts, D. F. (2010). *Generation M2: Media in the lives of 8- to 18-year-olds.* Menlo Park, CA: Kaiser Family Foundation.

Roediger, H. L., & Karpicke, J. D. (2006). Test enhanced learning: Taking memory tests improves long-term retention. *Psychological Sciences, 17*(3), 249–255.

Rose, L. C., & Gallup, A. M. (2007). The 39th annual Phi Delta Kappa/Gallup poll of the public's attitudes toward the public schools. *Phi Delta Kappan, 89*(1), 33–48.

Rosenstone, S. J. (2005). Education and America in the 21st century. Presentation to American Association of University Women. Retrieved November 29, 2010, from http://www.learnmoremn.org/userFiles/File/facts/Rosenstone_2005_AAUW_talk.pdf

Rothstein, R., Jacobsen, R., & Wilder, T. (2008). *Grading education: Getting accountability right.* New York and Washington, DC: Economic Policy Institute and Teachers College Press.

Russell, M., Bebell, D., & Higgins, J. (2004). Laptop learning: A comparision of teaching and learning in upper elementary classrooms equipped with shared carts of laptops and permanent 1:1 laptops. *Journal of Educational Computing Research, 30*(4), 313–330.

Sandholtz, J. H., Ringstaff, C., & Dwyer, D. C. (1997). *Teaching with technology: Creating student-centered classrooms.* New York: Teachers College Press.

Salen, K., Torres, R., Wolozin, L., Rufo-Tepper, R., & Shapiro, A. (2011). *Quest to Learn: Developing the school for digital kids.* Cambridge, MA: MIT Press.

Schwartz, D. L., & Bransford, J. D. (1998). A time for telling. *Cognition and Instruction, 16,* 475–522.

Schwartz, D. L., & Martin, T. (2004). Invention to prepare for future learning: The hidden efficiency of encouraging original student production in statistics instruction. *Cognition and Instruction, 22,* 129–184.

Shaffer, D. W., & Gee, J. P. (2005). *Before every child is left behind: How epistemic games can solve the coming crisis in education.* WCER Working Paper No 2005-7. Madison, WI: Wisconsin Center for Education Research.

Shulman, J. (1986). Those who understand: Knowledge growth in teaching. *Educational Researcher, 15*(2), 4–14.

Skinner, B. F. (1958). Teaching machines. *Science, 128*(3330), 969–977.

Slotta, J. D., & Linn, M. (2009). *WISE Science: Web-based inquiry in the classroom.* New York: Teachers College Press.

Smith, A., & Rainie, L. (2010). *8% of online Americans use Twitter.* Washington, DC: Pew Internet & American Life Project.

Spandel, V. (2009). *Creating writers through 6-train writing* (5th ed.). Boston: Pearson.

Spires, H. A., Wiebe, E., Young, C. A., Hollebrands, K., & Lee, J. K. (2009). *Toward a new learning ecology: Teaching and learning in 1:1 environments.* Raleigh, NC: Friday Institute for Educational Innovation, North Carolina State University.

Star, S. L., & Ruhleder, K. (1996). Steps toward an ecology of infrastructure: Design and access for large information spaces. *Information Systems Research, 7*(1), 111–134.

State of California. (2009). Gov. Schwarzenegger releases free digital textbook initiative Phase 1 report. Retrieved December 9, 2010, from http://gov.ca.gov/press-release/12996/

State of Maine Department of Education. (2010). Maine NECAP Test Results. Retrieved March 23, 2011, from http://www.maine.gov/education/necap/archive/2009results.html

Stilwell, R. (2010). *Public school graduates and dropouts from the common core of data: School year 2007–2008 (NCES 2010-341).* Washington, DC: National Center for Education Statistic, Institute of Education Sciences, U.S. Department of Education. Retrieved March 23, 2011, from http://nces.ed.gov/

Task Force on the Maine Learning Technology Endowment. (2001). *Teaching and learning for tomorrow: A learning technology plan for Maine's future.* Report to the State of Maine 119th Leglislature Second Regular Session. Retrieved November 25, 2010, from http://maine.gov/mlti/resources/history/mlterpt.pdf

Texas Center for Educational Research. (2009). Evaluation of the Texas Technology Immersion Pilot: Final outcomes for a four-year study (2004–2005 to 2007–2008). Austin: Author.

Tienken, C. H. (2010). Common core state standards: I wonder? *Kappa Delta Pi Record,* Fall, 14–17.

Toyama, K. (2010). Can technology end poverty? *Boston Review, 35*(6). Retrieved March 23, 2011, from http://bostonreview.net/BR35.6/toyama.php

U.S. Census Bureau. (2010). Mean earnings by highest degree earned: 2007. Retrieved November 29, 2010, from http://www.census.gov/

U.S. Department of Education. (2010). U.S. Secretary of Education Duncan announces winners of competition to improve student assessments. Retrieved December 21, 2010, from http://www.ed.gov/news/press-releases/

Vigdor, J. L., & Ladd, H. F. (2010). *Scaling the digital divide: Home computer technology and student achievement.* NBER Working Paper No. 16078. Retrieved June 21, 2010, from http://www.nber.org/papers/w16078

Vygotsky, L. S. (1978). *Mind and society.* Cambridge, MA: Harvard University Press.

Walker, R., & Vogel, C. (2005, June). Live Ink: Brain-based text formatting raises standardized test scores. Paper presented at the National Educational Computing Conference, Philadelphia.

Walker, R. C. (2007). Visual-syntactic text formatting: Theoretical basis and empirical evidence for impact on human reading. Paper presented at the IEEE Professional Communication Conference, 2007, Seattle. Retrieved from http://ieeexplore.ieee.org

Walker, S., Schloss, P., Fletcher, C. R., Vogel, C. A., & Walker, R. C. (2005). Visual-syntactic text formatting: A new method to enhance online reading. *Reading Online, 8*(6). Retrieved March 23, 2011 from http://www.readingonline.org/

Warschauer, M. (1999). *Electronic literacies: Language, culture, and power in online education.* Mahwah, NJ: Lawrence Erlbaum Associates.

Warschauer, M. (2000). Technology and school reform: A view from both sides of the track. *Education Policy Analysis Archives, 8*(4). Retrieved March 23, 2011 from http://epaa.asu.edu/epaa/v8n4.html

Warschauer, M. (2003). *Technology and social inclusion: Rethinking the digital divide.* Cambridge, MA: MIT Press.

Warschauer, M. (2006). *Laptops and literacy: Learning in the wireless classroom.* New York: Teachers College Press.

Warschauer, M., & Ames, M. (2010). Can One Laptop per Child save the world's poor? *Journal of International Affairs, 64*(1), 33–51.

Warschauer, M., & Grimes, D. (2007). Audience, authorship, and artifact: The emergent semiotics of Web 2.0. *Annual Review of Applied Linguistics, 27,* 1–23.

Warschauer, M., Knobel, M., & Stone, L. (2004). Technology and equity in schooling: Deconstructing the digital divide. *Educational Policy, 18*(4), 562–588.

Warschauer, M., & Matuchniak, T. (2010). New technology and digital worlds: Analyzing evidence of equity in access, use, and outcomes. *Review of Research in Education, 34*(1), 179–225.

Webster, T. (2010). Twitter usage in America: 2010. Retrieved May 25, 2010, from http://www.edisonresearch.com/

Wenglinsky, H. (1998). Does it compute?: The relationship between educational technology and student achievement in mathematics. Retrieved February 2, 2006, from ftp://ftp.ets.org/pub/res/technolog.pdf

Wenglinsky, H. (2005). *Using technology wisely: The keys to success in schools.* New York: Teachers College Press.

Wiggins, G. (1989). Teaching to the (authentic) test. *Educational Leadership, 41*(1), 41–46.

Wiggins, G., & McTighe, J. (1998). *Understanding by design.* Alexandria, VA: Association of Supervision and Curriculum Development.

Wiggins, G., & McTighe, J. (2007). *Schooling by design.* Alexandria, VA: Association of Supervision and Curriculum Development.

Willingham, D. T. (2009). *Why students don't like school: A cognitive scientist answers questions about how the mind works and what it means for the classroom.* San Francisco: Jossey-Bass.

Index

About the Author

Mark Warschauer is a professor of Education and Informatics at the University of California, Irvine, where he directs both the Ph.D. in Education program and the Digital Learning Lab. He has previously taught or conducted research at the University of Hawaii, Waseda University in Japan, Charles University in Prague, and Moscow State Linguistic University, and served as director of educational technology on a U.S. development project in Egypt. Warschauer is the author or editor of nine books and more than 100 papers on technology and learning, including *Laptops and Literacy: Learning in the Wireless Classroom* (Teachers College Press, 2006) and *Technology and Social Inclusion: Rethinking the Digital Divide* (MIT Press, 2003). His research on these topics has been funded by the National Science Foundation, the Haynes Foundation, the Mott Foundation, Cambridge University, and Google. Previously, he served as founding editor of *Language Learning & Technology* journal and received the Educational Testing Service/TOEFL Policy Council Language Acquisition and Instruction International Award for outstanding individual contribution in the area of technology and language learning. Warschauer lives in Irvine, California, with his wife and three children.